THE AWAKENING

Fear, Freedom & Vaccines

Dear Waqar
To my dear Fatima:
Always ask questions &
take a stand for
what you believe
is true
[illegible]

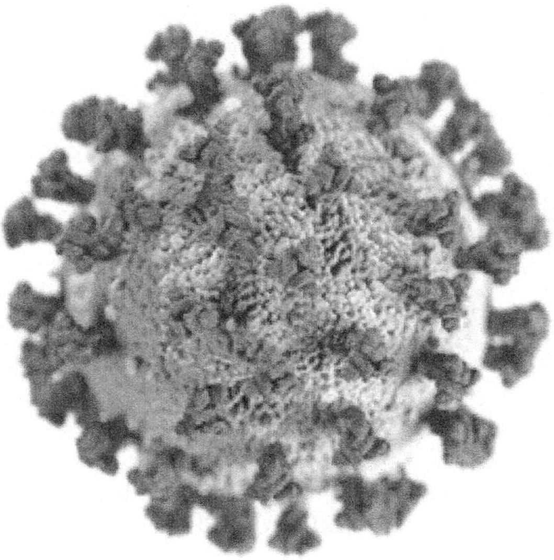

The Awakening

Fear, Freedom & Vaccines

TED HILL

The Awakening: Fear, Freedom & Vaccines
By Ted Hill

ISBN: 978-1-956193-02-2
Book Design & Publishing done by:
Susmita Dutta
Global Book Publishing
www.globalbookpublishing.com

Disclaimer: The Publisher and the Authors make no representations or warranties with respect to the accuracy and completeness of this work and specially disclaim all warranties, including without limitation warranties of fitness for a particular purpose. No warranty may be created or extended by sales or promotional materials. The advice and strategies contain herein may not be suitable for every situation. This work is sold with the understanding that the Publisher is not engaged in rendering legal, accounting, or other professional services. If professional assistance is required, the services of a competent professional person should be sought. Neither the Publisher nor the Author shall be liable for the damages arising here from. Then fact that an organization or website is referred to in this work as a citation or potential source of further information does not mean that the Author or the Publisher endorses the information the organization or the website may provide or recommendations it may make. Further, readers should be aware that internet websites listed in this work may have changed or disappeared between when this work was written and when it is used.

This book is dedicated to any and all people who have taken a stand. Whether it was in the performance of their duties like our front line workers or those doctors and scientists who risked their career going against the establishment by using early treatments ultimately saving thousands of lives.
More importantly, those who took some form of action against an unwarranted lockdown with our freedom and liberties being taken away.

Table of Contents

1

The Awakening to Hypocrisy as the New Normal

"Hypocrites get offended by the truth."

—Jess C. Scott

- Largest Human Behaviour Study
- What Really Been Exposed
- Is Better Health The New Outcome

Chapter 1

Vaccines have been touted as the holy grail of medicine, the greatest achievement of all time, and an explanation for the global decline of infectious diseases. This pandemic has now put vaccines on the table to provide a chance for all to truly examine their track record and why there is a lack of transparency on serious adverse events? True advances in medicine, vaccines, and such as newfangled innovative medical procedures, have saved millions of lives. When we're ill, our doctors truly become our saviors. Around the globe, vaccines have and continue to save untold souls. We must thank the WHO, pharmaceutical corporations, governments, doctors, and Bill Gates. These entities are reducing disease and saving lives with effective vaccines.

It's true but there is another side to this that is not being told and that has been hidden. The pandemic (or the reaction by health advisors and politicians), has opened up Pandora's box when it comes to vaccines. Pharmaceutical companies certainly benefit from their 'end game' but now there is exposure. If the Health and Human Services Harvard Pilgrim investigation showed that "fewer than 1% of vaccine adverse events" are reported, what would 99% more look like? It would be huge.

How did a miracle happen to produce a vaccine in record time? How did Moderna who has not developed any vaccines for public use get clinical trials underway just 6 weeks after lockdown? The vax has an efficacy factor of 95%, but very few really understand what that really means.

It seems the mandate is to keep introducing new vaccines to protect all of us in the world from the untold raging diseases. It's getting to a point if there is a disease we can create a vaccine.

Sars Cov 2 and the infection COVID-19 is real. Whether or not it originated in the Wuhan Lab, the virus has impacted the globe. The global lockdowns have been well synchronized, but leaders, scientists, and politicians around the globe continue to deliver contradictory messages. We are told we need to listen to the science, we don't have enough data, that Covid is a moving target and we are learning and the same with the vaccines. Endless contradictions on everything, including the science. Then the long list of the hysterical waking up each day getting a case and death report, whether you can go outside or not, sit at a table with another as long as one person has had at least 1 jab, one is wearing two masks, had a negative PCR test at least 3 days before, only talking quietly and the next day it all changes.

The question is 'have we all been duped by the lockdown'? There is an acronym that best describes the actions of a lockdown: FEAR–F. alse E.vidence A.ppearing R.eal. Another acronym might be TEAR–T. rue E.vidence A.ppearing R.eal in the role of some major players Facebook, Amazon, Google, and Gates in the vaccine space. We all need to replace fear with knowledge.

Mers, Sars, and H1N1 viruses all impacted our older population and those with pre-existing conditions. Why didn't we learn about how to protect our seniors? Vaccines, as we all know, are supposed to prevent disease. These new vaccines do not. Nor do they prevent transmission. But the good news is that there are 90 vaccines in different trial stages for the annual boosters[1] to come to combat the new variants and the plan to get 6-month-old babies to 11 years vaxxed. Unlike the flu shot which was by choice, the Covid vaccine narrative has subjected us to relentless pestering and weakened our spirit.

[1]https://thehighwire.com/videos/boosters-proving-vaccine-isnt-effective

It has been mandated not directly but in the form of removing rights and freedoms and if you want them back get vaxxed. How does any parent accept our health advisors to our government allowing a 12-year-old to decide on their own without parent knowledge to get the vaccine? Why not take a pause and learn about the benefit versus risk to this age group? How much ice cream does it take? There is no evidence that this age group is at risk. Where is the informed consent? Isn't this totally unethical? On the WHO website, it reads do not vaccinate 12–18-year-olds. In fact, 18-plus adults there is a high number of myocarditis events which some will not recover from. There is a reason why this is not being reported on the mainstream news. The mantra with vaccines is and continues to be is there may be a correlation but not causation. The data from the under reported US Vaccine Adverse Event Reporting System as of mid-July 2021 shows 2800 deaths within 48 hours after the vaccine and 3900 over other time periods. A further 30k hospitalizations. Flu vaccines have been pulled with just 50 deaths?

VAERS government-funded systems require further investigation before a causal relationship can be confirmed.

UK-native Professor Neil Ferguson kicked off the pandemonium with his model projection of 4% global population deaths, which sent governments around the world into a panic. Everyone has experienced the immediate and extensive aftermath to varying degrees. The fear has been seen in people's eyes amidst the mask frenzy.

How morbid has it been to constantly hear case and death numbers as politician's demand that we remain under lockdown? Then, to have this reinforced by seeing everyone with a mask. Seeing the fear when the mask drops below the nose. A fear so strong that some otherwise intelligent, reasonable, logical, and open-minded people had become aggressive, and as a result stress levels were up with fights and in fact deaths.

Add to the equation social deprivation, economic fallout, and social upheaval.

Many things, we're told, in science, are not exactly as they appear. We're told as much repeatedly for long enough that we finally take it as fact, however absurd because it is human nature.

Effectively, we have been brainwashed, and we are simply accepting it. No one thinks they are brainwashed. The term *brainwash*, defined by Cambridge Dictionary sounds strikingly familiar to what we have been subjected to: "to make someone believe something by repeatedly telling them that it is true and preventing any other information from reaching them." In addition, there has been misinformation coming from all sources including trusted authorities supported by the tech giants that have decided what we should believe. Take, for example, parents buying into the narrative their children need the vaccine and yet the risk of serious adverse events from the vaccine are far greater than not getting the vaccine. This is the data. This is the reality for parents who keep their children in a bubble in a pristine environment. Don't play in the dirt, don't get your hands dirty–nature is dangerous.

Why are people who present facts—even facts that come from the FDA or CDC website that are publicly available to anyone willing to do the research and connect the dots—being banned? Why the extent of the level of censorship and labeling of content from social media platforms like YouTube, Facebook, and Twitter?

What could explain Big Pharma's drive and mission to have a vaccine for every disease? We are getting very close to 90 doses of vaccines from the CDC schedule before the age of 18. Covid 19 and the boosters to follow will get us closer. Not every disease needs to be challenged. Take, for example, if you travel to Japan they recommend the vaccine for Japanese encephalitis. The total number of deaths over the years has been 12. The deaths from the vaccine they created are over 200. But they still recommend you get it. Whose to know? What could explain the massive pipeline of vaccines in different stages of trial or the push for mandatory vaccines?

Now they want to achieve herd immunity via experimental vaccines with unknown long-term side effects, all the while barring test subjects the legal right to sue the manufacturers for injuries.

Is it the goal to integrate technology into the human body using mandatory vaccinations as the entry point? Perhaps yes, when you look at the full picture. This is already happening with embedded applications on RFID chips. Is the goal, then, to be connected to big data analytics no longer a choice? Sadly, this would appear so.

They have been inculcating the belief that the only way to return to normalcy is through a vaccine designed by the very companies they've invested in.

In January of 2021, Bill Gates stated that, "We must prepare for the next pandemic like we prepare for war." A month later, headlines read: "Bill Gates warns that the next pandemic could be ten times worse." Bill has been accused of predicting this pandemic and now he is on to the next one. Perhaps, if someone establishes enough fear, takeaway your freedom and only give them back if you take an experimental vaccine.

Why is he so involved with vaccines? Why does he top the charts when it comes to conspiracy theories? How is it that Bill Gates became a medical spokesperson getting more media bandwidth than scientists? Does this sound like the start of positioning a major global agenda? Yes, and it is not hidden either.

There is no exact scientific data in concluding how much less deadly the common flu is than COVID-19 except data is now showing from reliable sources it is more akin to a severe flu and not on a pandemic level to warrant the extreme lockdown. Those sources are the CDC, Tony Fauci, and scientists from around the globe. ICAN, the Informed Consent Action Network who are pro-truth about vaccine transparency received thousands of Tony Fauci emails through the Freedom of Information Act. This is the start of the truth coming out. It explains his flip-flop on the effectiveness of masks, just how severe Covid is or is not, and his connection through the NIH (National Institute of Health) the funding of Covid virus research with the Wuhan Lab. And certainly lays out a roadmap for a much bigger agenda.

- CDC does not know exactly how many people die from the seasonal flu each year. There is no regulation involved in reporting that the flu was the cause of death for over the age of eighteen, is infrequently listed on death certificates and many flu-related deaths occur one or two weeks after a person's initial infection. This is because it may have aggravated an existing chronic illness. Also, most people who die from flu-related complications are not tested for influenza. But that process changed completely with Covid 19. In some cases, if someone died through observation one could assume Covid was a factor and notate it on the death certificate.

- CDC and other public health agencies in the United States and other countries use statistical and mathematical models to estimate the annual number of flu-related deaths.
- Since 2010, the data collected through FluSurv-NET has provided estimates indicating that the flu has resulted in between 140,000 and 960,000 hospitalizations each year.
- COVID-19 deaths for many countries are listed as "died with COVID-19, not "died from COVID-19." CDC for the US actual numbers are 6% of deaths are directly caused by Covid.

Is the data strong enough to warrant global lockdowns?

At this point, world leaders are openly talking about the great reset.

The World Economic Forum Agenda states on their website: "You will own nothing and you will be happy." The elite believe that this is brilliant because they, the super-rich, will own even more and be happier than ever.

There are larger voices out there like–Great Barrington Declaration[2]. Mainstream media will not present this on their news. Over fifty thousand doctors and scientists have signed the Declaration, which commits to simply following previous protocols on how to deal with a pandemic.

Locking down billions of people, causing vast damage to the economy; harming children's mental health; causing deaths of despair; and destroying businesses is far worse than targeted shielding.

The virus is harmless to the vast majority. Herd immunity was always standard practice in civilized democratic and liberal societies. Lockdowns were imported from China.

Once natural immunity was achieved, it would have been safer for the vulnerable to mix again with greater society—a far less damaging, far more compassionate approach.

[2]https://gbdeclaration.org

Instead, we have Facebook cracking down on what they believe is "misinformation," including top leading scientists who continue to state that they don't know if such measures do anything to prevent asymptomatic infection, furthermore questioning if the vaccines are effective against the diseases they are meant to prevent.

Many top doctors have voices that are not being listened to.

Dr. Robert Malone[3] who invented the mRNA vaccine has been calling for a stop to the mRNA vaccine.

Dr. Hooman Noorchashm, a surgeon, immunologist, and patient safety advocate said it's a colossal error to vaccinate people who have previously had COVID.

Dr. Mike Yeardon, previous Chief Scientific Officer for Allergy and Respiratory Research–Pfizer for 13 years believes governments are being misguided on PCR tests, the lockdown, and the vaccine.

Dr. Stefan Baral and Dr. Vinay Prasad published in the British Medical Journal challenge the benefit of the vaccine to children "given the rarity of severe clinical courses and limited clarity of risks, the criteria for emergency use authorization do not appear to be met for children."

Dr. John Ianidis, an epidemiologist from Stanford University, believes Covid is a bad flu and the actual danger is a continuance of fear.

"While we should take the outbreak seriously, we mustn't panic and behave in a manner that is disproportionate to the threat we are confronted with," said Annelies Wilder-Smith, a professor of emerging infectious diseases at the London School of Hygiene and Tropical Medicine.

There are thousands of other very brilliant people speaking out but the media and government will not acknowledge.

There seem to be unlimited diseases: mumps, chickenpox, the flu, and diseases like measles. But what really hurts is the litany of more serious, debilitating, and costly long-term chronic illnesses plaguing our society and threatening to exhaust our Health Care Systems, bankrupting our economies.

[3]https://thehighwire.com/videos/episode-221-the-mrna-insider

What is your level of confidence in what you've been told about vaccines by the pharmaceutical industry, the media, your doctor, and the government?

The censorship team deploys fact-checking organizations to make it look like they are providing you accurate information. They take information, take a statement out of context, label it misinformation–False. They even state what their go-to websites are for accuracy.

Three websites met fact-checkers' approval and inclusion criteria for trusted information: Cochrane Evidence, Informed Health, and PubMed Health. My fact checking and research has involved more than fifty sources and many became moving targets.

My research for this book has taken me down the proverbial rabbit hole. The true story needs like a whole encyclopedia to explain. The rabbit hole became more like the story I read decades ago about authority, oppression, surveillance, obedience when the sky is falling–the book *Watership Down* by Richard Adams.

Watership Down recounts the travels of a group of rabbits searching for their "forever home"—a place where they will be free from oppression and fear, and able to live as they please in harmony with both nature and one another.

Watership Down has been described as the timeless struggle between tyranny and freedom; reason and blind conformity by the people from the government; and the individual and the corporate state.

Myxomatosis (Covid19) is referred to as "the white blindness," and all rabbits who seem to be afflicted by this disease are driven out by the chief.

The rabbit in control is General Woundwort, who develops systems of control. He devises the Marks, each controlled by its own officers and sentries, which stipulate feeding times and how much sunshine will be received. All signs of rabbit life and interactions are concealed and controlled as much as possible. Privileges are granted regarding feeding, mating, and freedom of movement. Any failure of duty is liable to be punished by demotion and loss of privileges. For ordinary rabbits, the punishments are even more severe.

While Watership Down is symbolic of democracy in action, General Woundwort, is symbolic of authoritarianism and fascism. But in the end, democracy, rights, and freedom of choice win out.

In our world today, this is a true parallel in this crisis. We are not rabbits. We are not sheep although many people would differ. But if we continue to listen to the mainstream media (General Woundwart) as the basis for our understanding—if we allow them to formulate our perspective by bombarding the narrative on an hourly basis, pushing us to harass neighbors who don't wear a mask—then we have the white blindness. "Listen to the science" "wash your hands" 'stay six feet apart" haves been common phrases.

The Doctors Of Today

The doctors of today practice conventional medicine: a system in which healthcare professionals treat symptoms and diseases using drugs, radiation, and/or surgery. And they are very good at what they do, as long as their patients are seeing them for an acute medical condition.

They are trained to diagnose and prescribe medication. They are not trained to effectively treat chronic diseases through lifestyle medicine.

Conditions such as type 2 diabetes, heart disease, and obesity, are brought on by poor lifestyle choices, such as tobacco use, lack of physical activity, and poor eating habits. And the majority of chronic diseases can be prevented and reversed through healthy lifestyle choices.

The doctors of today specialize in short-term care, such as a broken leg or bronchitis. But the patients of today require a different kind of care. Today, 45% of patients have at least one chronic disease. A chronic disease is one lasting three months or more and generally cannot be cured by vaccines or medication.

The Doctors Of The Future

Doctors of the future already exist. They practice functional medicine. Functional medicine trains practitioners to treat the body as one integrated system. It empowers healthcare providers to treat the root cause of disease, instead of symptoms, through lifestyle modifications.

The result can be the reversal of chronic disease; patients who look, move, and feel better; and a healthcare system that focuses on optimal health, rather than the mere absence of disease.

The doctors of the future are trained to empower patients to make the necessary lifestyle changes to prevent and reverse their illnesses.

Why would I ever question vaccine safety? Why would you? They have generally proven safe and effective. It's true, they have saved millions of lives. Our parents went along with the system. The system was pushed forward by pharma, by government, and by institutions all insisting that vaccines are important to keep disease under control.

Here is one analogy. Driving cars is safe and effective, but the risks are well known by all.

There is a love affair people have with cars. Safety standards are high, and we're afforded the freedom to go anywhere we want. Anyone who drives a vehicle would understand that cars today are, indeed, very safe and it is the driver that causes the accident 99% of the time. I'm sure someone somewhere has mathematically worked out how many lives cars have saved each year. So, saved lives how exactly?

For such a study to exist, they would have to do a large study, taking forty thousand people from around the world, for example (similar to a recent vaccine study). Then, they would allow half to drive and designate the other half as the control group or placebo who don't drive, how many in each group would die from car accidents? It is totally obvious what the results would be if such a study was ever conducted.

The reason we don't ask what the risks are of driving a car is that we know them. A split second could lead to disaster, but we assume that risk, thinking we are safe as long as we're personally careful.

Some Vital Stats: The average is four accidents per person throughout their lifetime. The CDC reports that in any three-year period, four million people are killed on roadways around the world—or about 14,300 people are killed globally in crashes each day. WHO states that between sixty and one hundred fifty million more people suffer non-fatal injuries, with many incurring a disability as a result of their injury.

And we thought vaccines might be risky? No vaccines are 100% safe and 100% effective. But just like driving, there is a risk. So, what are those risks? The mainstream science says they have done studies. There are other peer-reviewed scientists with different viewpoints.

If you or someone you know has been impacted, you know the risk. The risk may be more than just a flare-up on your arm after vaxxing. The damage may be revealed ten or twenty years later in the form of a chronic disease. How would you know?

How do you think a study is done? The CDC states that they apply the gold standard of testing and mainstream news reassures us of that. But what is the Gold Standard?

In a world deluged by irrelevant information, clarity is power. Censorship works not just by blocking the flow of information but, rather, by flooding people with disinformation and distractions.

What can we do about the epidemic of fake news?

No one can hardly afford the luxury of in-depth investigating and researching these matters because we have more pressing things to do: we have to go to work, take care of the kids, or look after elderly parents.

This book doesn't give solutions to solve world issues. It is not a scientific journal but it is supported by scientific documentation, fact checked by scientific studies on reputable websites like The Lancet, PubMed, British Medical Journal, and the CDC to name just a few. It does, however, offer awareness—some clarity regarding where we're not being told about vaccines. If this book empowers even a handful of people to ask questions, join the debate, expose information that's been covered up, and face the reality of what might happen with the next vaccine given to you, your children, or your grandchildren, it has done its job.

The exaggerated reporting, the inflated death rates, and the rest of it have perfectly set the stage to stoke fears and dissolve freedoms.

What this has done, however, is create newfound awareness of corruption. Overall, many believe in the need for an exhaustive independent investigation regarding the safety and effectiveness of vaccines, mass corruption, the pharmaceutical industry, the FDA, and the CDC.

It certainly won't be the first time anyone has heard about corruption within the highest levels of corporate and government. In a vaccine world, there is a revolving door within all these groups, and conflict of interest abounds. People at the highest levels including Tony Fauci and billionaires with interests in patents for vaccines. It is the reason why the CDC and pharmaceutical companies should not be in charge of the neutral and unbiased research that needs to be done on vaccines. So far, sadly, they've called the shots.

Every day, it is cases, deaths, masks, booster vaccines, and unlimited misinformation, all perfectly orchestrated to produce one outcome: fear. Only you can control what you do, how you live, and how you want to control your life.

There is no bad guy out there making us mask or isolate our children. There is no bad guy locking us in our homes. There is no bad guy injecting us and our children. There is no bad guy ruining the businesses that we worked for generations to build. We are doing these things to ourselves. This means we have the power and the agency to stop these practices. Because more is coming.

The Extreme Of Lockdown

We can't bury our dead? We can't attend a funeral? We can't attend to our spouse/child in the hospital on their deathbed? We have to talk to our beloved parents (who in many cases are left alone) via devices. Now, the aim to vaccinate 6mth old children to protect them from Covid and the variants. It's wholly inhuman and unethical.

We had Sars in 2002, and it was gone two years—no vaccine, no herd immunity—and the same held true of Mers in 2012. Gone by the end of 2013.

Over twelve thousand viruses have been discovered since 1976. In reality, there are hundreds of thousands of known viruses. We've seen them as prompts on the news and we know so much more about our immune system, T-Cells, and spike proteins.

What is in the air and soil is far beyond what a supercomputer could estimate. We are genomic machines. We are surrounded by genomic information. We breathe in viruses and exhale viruses.

A New Virus?

Our planet has gone through cataclysmic events, from ice ages to years of volcanic activity. Today, humankind is the cataclysmic event.

We should be far from startled to see the decline of our health. But let's do it with Eyes Wide Open.

There is a genomic language predicated on viruses. They are the very language of life. We have been told that viruses are the enemy, but they're perfectly natural.

By way of example, weeds in your garden represent the collapse of biodiversity. Similarly, in the areas where these outbreaks occur, you'll find a complete breakdown of biodiversity. Weeds are effectively the building blocks of recreating the biodiversity that was there.

Any microbe will find its way.

Viruses find their way in damaged ecosystem. When eight thousand people were sampled, it was discovered that they had microbes of forty-two viruses, including HIV.

We're scratching the surface of genomic modification, but the point is clear: Mother Nature can do anything ten thousand times faster than we can. Adaptability conquers all.

What we are trying to do is create joint modifications or medicine to stop viruses for capitalistic reasons, when Mother Nature does it naturally.

Why the high death count in the US? Co-morbidity and chronic issues. The US has the highest medicalized system in the world with 54% of citizens suffering chronic conditions. Wasn't there some science learned from H1N1, Mers, Sars, and annual influenza?

CDC knows that science. The National Institute of Health (NIH) knows. So, why did we not make public health moves to protect the vulnerable? Look at one of the first outbreaks on that cruise ship. For fourteen days, they were quarantined on the Oakland cruise ship in March. The average age was over seventy, so they were in the highest risk category for issues, so there should have been a major death toll, but there were none. That outbreak should have 'flooded the deck' in cases and deaths!

Framework To Roll Out Vaccines

So, what do I mean by a "framework?" Start with the basic assumption that there is an agenda to roll out as many vaccines as possible under mandatory rules and those who believe they should be excluded face extreme penalties. No work policy. Stay at home mandatory. Freedom/travel restrictions.

Okay, seems to be a bit on the far side. Yes, today it is but not when you look at the groundwork that has been laid by government, pharma, vaccine patent ownership, CDC, and Bill Gates. Of course, that look may take you months to review.

Planning for mandatory vaccines and vaccine passports has been in the works for a long time. And now there is the groundwork to make it happen with this pandemic.

Trigger Criteria For Vaccination Mandates

The New England Journal of Medicine (NEJM), which is known for being amongst the most prestigious medical journals in the world, argues that state governments need a "strategy" for deploying the coming COVID-19 vaccine—meaning making it mandatory. Because only 51% of US citizens plan to get the vaccine.

One condition is providing evidence that COVID-19 presents an "ongoing threat" to the state, explaining that the threat could be demonstrated by "sustained troubling trends in new cases, hospitalizations, or deaths." (Naturally, the media would be happy to oblige.)

A "generous compensation program for people who have serious vaccine side effects." Why? Because it may not be safe and effective and did not adhere to the gold standard of testing. But then again, no vaccine has adhered fully to the said CDC /FDA gold standard (Hmmn, that's a bold statement, I heard they always do the Gold Standard). The question of why state governments should mandate a vaccine it expects to induce serious side effects is unanswered in the article.

What has happened is that everyone has been impacted each one of us having their own awakening. Hypocrisy at every level, flip flop, the science, and most importantly, the narrative from the media has presented a new perspective. So, what is it that we are not being told? Why the extreme censorship and what are the connections with the powerful pharmaceutical companies, media, and big tech?

2

The Birth of Pharma & The Scandals that Followed

"The doctor of the future will give no medicine, but will interest his patient in the care of the human frame, in diet, and in the cause and prevention of disease."

—Thomas Edison

- Germ Theory
- Attack On Natural Healing
- Pandemic Bigger Than Covid

Chapter 2

So, Mr. Edison, what happened?

Germ Theory Won & It Was The Birth Of Pharma

Let us look at the major turning point of natural health and healing to that how medicine alone has taken over. The true meaning today here is when you see your doctor you do not get a prescription for natural healing.

In the mid-1850s, Louis Pasteur's germ theory and Antoine Bechamp's microzymian principle would come to represent two scientific theories—one of which the direction that medicine would take.

Germ theory is about microorganisms known as pathogens, or "germs", that can lead to disease. These small organisms invade humans, other animals, and other living hosts, reproduce within their hosts and can cause disease. The germ theory quickly led to the identification of the actual organisms that cause many diseases.

Bechamp proposed that tiny organisms (opposed to cells) are the fundamental building block of life—the foundation of all life and life processes on Earth. Bechamp's term for these lifeforms was microzymas, and he claimed they are present in all things—animal, vegetable, and mineral—whether living or dead. In a state of health, the microzymas act harmoniously and our life is, in every meaning of the word, balanced. In the condition of disease, the microzymas do not act harmoniously, their function being changed by food, environment, wellbeing, or genetic factors. Means of treatment include alternative medicine: naturalistic, holistic, acupuncture, and more.

Bechamp's ideas did not gain acceptance, and Pasteur's germ theory won. By the early 1900s, insulin and penicillin discoveries created a clear pathway for the world of major pharma companies. The world of medicine became health-driven but tenfold profit-driven.

The Great Sanitary Awakening

The identification of filth as both a cause of disease and a vehicle of transmission—and the ensuing embrace of cleanliness—was a central component of nineteenth-century social reform. Sanitation changed the way society thought about health. Illness came to be seen as an indicator of poor social and environmental conditions, as well as poor moral and spiritual conditions. Cleanliness was embraced as a path both to physical and moral health. Cleanliness, piety, and isolation were seen to be compatible and mutually reinforcing measures to help the public resist disease.

Rockefellers/Carnegie

They were the donors and with control of the funding to medical institutions, shadowy interests could eliminate competition to the progress of patented chemicals or medicines, thus influencing and reporting on the medical institutions that were not practicing what they felt was sound (i.e., lucrative) medical information.

Carnegie & Rockefeller began pouring millions of dollars into the medical schools that were teaching drug-intensive medicine. After becoming large donors, they would place a member of one of their foundations on the board to see how money was being spent, and of course, pushed for more pharmaceutical drugs.

Thousands of herbal, natural medicine, and holistic businesses were closed and ostracized, for their natural teaching and healing were being prosecuted. The natural healing schools started to close as well, and by 1950, virtually none remained.

The Immune System

So now, the world is being educated about the immune system. Your immune system thrives on what you eat, breathe, drink, and what is injected.

The human body is an immune system. Everyone on the planet has heard it at least once and others thousands of times. Yes, we are, in a sense, a virus.

More accurately, the human corpus represents a system composed of viruses, bacteria, fungi, parasites, and a few human elements too.

The last decade has uncovered discoveries of the vast universe science calls "the microbiome." Two paradigm-shifting conclusions have been ascertained from thousands of research studies: neither human immunity nor the human brain function without the interaction of millions of species of tiny organisms that inhabit every niche of the human body. Why is this all going to be important? Because what we eat and more importantly what we get injected with impacts all the cells in our bodies that prevent disease.

And the majority of the microbiome is in the gut. Every internal organ—including the liver, kidneys, vascular system, and brain—has unique ecosystems of viruses: bacteria and fungi that maintain balance and function.

The foundation of the gut and microbiome in human health cannot be overemphasized. Your gut lining is composed of a super-thin cellophane-like barrier—not so much a wall as an intelligent gatekeeper, allowing the good stuff in and keeping out unwanted toxins, organic, and inorganic matter.

In a profoundly eloquent method of checks and balances, Mother Nature has designed our gut barrier—the primary structure that defines self-identity at the biologic level—to be completely dependent on its continuous contact with the microbial population of the earth. Through your breath, food, and all you touch, your microbiome is an extension of you. If you isolate yourself from nature and its biodiversity, you will falter in your self-identity, immune function, and mind.

Neither the microbiome nor the virome is against us. The microbiome, communicating via viruses, is the origin of biologic life and the avenue of adaptation that makes a biodiverse abundant and resilient. If we fight it, we will die.

The human immune system is never out to kill bacteria and viruses. That is not its purpose. Its purpose is to bring you into balance with those organisms. You're supposed to have bacteria, fungi, and viruses in every niche of your body. If you were a sterilizing machine, you'd be dead. We are now using prescriptions and vaccines as a sterilizing machine.

The public is starting to realize that there's been a long play here, by the pharmaceutical industries as a whole, to start to really control human behavior for their own profit. Once you try to force people to use your product, however, you're going to fail.

People are inherently a creative species. They are striving for biological, psychological, philosophical, and ultimately spiritual freedom. You cannot suppress that stuff.

We are on that slippery path now, and the planet, as human beings start to strive for freedom that isn't just about not wearing a mask.

Our freedom pertains to thinking in the stream of consciousness of the universe for the first time. The new paradigm is one of freedom at the most fundamental level. So, are you going to throw a mask on tomorrow to go into the grocery store? Of course, you are—because it's not worth the fight. That's not the fight.

It is a common misconception that those who question modern vaccines are against all vaccines. The truth is that most skeptics understand that it's absolutely wonderful to have access to antibiotics when you need them—when they are being used appropriately.

One wouldn't want an antibiotic for a viral infection, and others would be remiss to call that person an "anti-antibiotic." But when people question vaccine safety and/or efficacy, they're attacked.

Meanwhile, much of the theory behind vaccines is lost, and we forget that what really keeps us healthy is a strong immune system.

So, is it possible to use your immune system specifically? Can you control some aspect of it so that you develop immunity to something that's causing harm? This goes back to the history of vaccinations—the idea of taking a little bit of something that was causing disease or that was similar to it and getting it under the skin. This can get your body to mount an immune response so that in the future when you got exposed to it, your body would be ready to prime the immune system.

Then, the organism that's been killed will be assessed by your body, which will recognize it and develop antibodies, so next time you're exposed, your immune system can react quickly and you won't actually get sick.

Regarding COVID-19, there are thousands of voices from other health institutions and doctors around the world who are not being heard about natural immunity. They are being silenced, censored, and the media is not giving them a platform, but a global pushback has begun.

Has Big Pharma has been waiting in the wings for something like this pandemic to happen? These corporations have been driving and pushing vaccines for the last thirty years, since the 1986 ACT which indemnifies all vaccine makers from lawsuits and it now becomes a gold rush to which company can provide the silver bullet—the unicorn—and vaccinate the world.

Many "conspiracies" are focused on government and espionage, and they prove far too complicated to unravel.

Conspiracy. Just saying the word in conversation can make people politely edge away, looking for someone who won't corner them with wild theories about how Elvis, John F. Kennedy, and Bigfoot are cryogenically frozen in an underground bunker.

Yet, conspiracies do exist. They most often are bundled in with collusion and conflict of interest. In the corporate world, major companies we buy products from every day have been found guilty of conspiring to fix prices and reduce competition. Pharmaceutical products have killed hundreds of thousands of people yet doctors still prescribed their product and we do what our doctor says.

Many conspiracy theorists go much further, though, and see a hidden hand behind the world's major events. While some of the theories have a grain of truth to them, conspiracy theories are impossible to disprove, because the hardcore believers will find some way to rationalize away evidence that contradicts their beliefs. Eyewitnesses who dispute their conclusions are mistaken—or part of the conspiracy themselves.

It's little wonder that Big Pharma is looked upon with suspicion. But it is more than suspicion. Hundreds of thousands of deaths by pharma have already been proven but we still go back to our Doctor without question for the next pill that will help. But some proponents of alternative medicine believe that drug companies actually conspire to keep people sick to reap profits.

Drugs cost too much, drug company profits are obscene, and it seems that every few months, some drug once claimed to be safe is yanked off the shelf after patients die.

For example, Kevin Trudeau (author of the bestselling *Natural Cures They Don't Want You To Know About*) claims that important medical information is being kept hidden by a conspiracy between the medical establishment and big drug companies.

According to Trudeau: "There are certain groups, including... the drug industry... that don't want people to know about cures for diseases..." Actress and model Jenny McCarthy appeared on Larry King Live, accusing doctors and the pharmaceutical industry of conspiring to suppress evidence of a link between childhood vaccines and autism.

But here's the thing. Conspiracies were and are happening right in front of us with our Eyes Wide Open. Suppression, censorship, and lack of media coverage and/or investigation can be observed all around us if your eyes are wide open.

The Opioid Crisis

It is by necessity that we continue to come back to companies to use products that kill us. Mainstream media only once in and a while reports this giving us the impression that pharma is 100% trustworthy. Nearly 500 thousand of Americans have died in an opioid epidemic that has its roots in the Food and Drug Administration's approval of the painkiller OxyContin and dishonest, aggressive marketing of the drug by its maker, Purdue Pharma. So much for long-term studies prior to FDA approval.

There have been thousands of opioid-related lawsuits nationwide, and a harsh reality is emerging: the money the pharmaceutical industry will pay to compensate ravaged communities will likely be far less than once envisioned.

Plaintiff lawyers believe the payout from dozens of opioid makers, distributors, and retailers is likely to be less than half of what the four Big Tobacco companies agreed to pay more than twenty years ago in a landmark settlement with states over costs associated with millions of smoking-related deaths.

The Tobacco Master Settlement Agreement in 1998 was originally spread out over the States, which were to receive over $206 billion payable over twenty-five years

The opioid crisis and the payment amount will certainly fall well short of what public health experts say is needed to heal the long-term effects of the opioid crisis: a mere $100 billion. Historic evidence has shown that if a settlement might cost a few billion and the pharma made tenfold than our shareholders have been rewarded in an unintentional tradeoff of the drug.

Estimates vary over just how much money it would take to finance the treatment, prevention programs, and all other measures needed to fix the problems created by opioids. The Federal Council of Economic Advisers estimated the economic toll from opioids was more than $2.5 trillion, including the cost of healthcare and law enforcement.

Further, the received funds for the majority of those states were used for other purposes and not the people they harmed.

The Catholic Conspiracy

This was a difficult story—one that proved almost untouchable at the time it broke. It was deemed to be heresy, as trust was put in the highest places. People who spoke of it were considered typical conspiracy theorists by those who have only one closed-minded perspective. But a handful of people still challenged it. Young boys were being abused by catholic priests. For decades, all the signs were there. The rumors—events that parents were ostracized for discussing. So many knew it was happening but did not want to confront the truth. This parallels with so many other situations including Covid.

Even the hierarchy of the church knew but dealt with parents by moving priests from one parish to another to hide the fact. The police and FBI wouldn't act. No publicity was given.

At some point, it had to be challenged, but who was going to take on religion? As it turned out: the Boston Globe. The fear of the church and people of faith in all occupations was that if this problem was exposed, then it would wreak havoc, shock belief systems, and cause a loss of faith affecting millions of people. The people at the top knew. The Catholic Church prioritized reputation over vulnerable children. The product of the study, titled the John Jay Report, indicated that some eleven thousand allegations had been made against 4,392 priests in the USA.

People of faith were rocked by their most trusted. The underlying point here is where do we place our trust? So is it possible that there is something similar with Covid 19? Of course. That in many businesses—from church to Big Tobacco to Big Pharma—the focus seems to be just on profit and image.

The Smoking Pandemic

Smoking does not cause cancer, and cigarettes are endorsed by doctors. All drugs and vaccines are safe and effective and prevent disease. The science and the studies on both accounts have been done and can be confirmed. So today health advisors say the Covid vaccine is safe and effective. That's all you need to know. What else it does to your cellular structure that might manifest into other medical ailments is unknown? Doctors believe that any reaction after getting a vaccine is just a coincidence. That the CDC has told them that correlation is not causation and there is no evidence to support otherwise.

Of course, most of the above is untrue. What can be learned by looking at this paradox?

Well, it may be an Awakening but Covid pales in comparison to what our health authorities allow for a known pandemic for decades. Globally, smoking will directly cause approximately eight million deaths this year. And that number is increasing. COVID-19 is at 3.5 million (at the time of this writing), and a large percentage of those is correlation (and that includes the majority of Covid related not caused by), not causation (per the CDC). Regardless, wouldn't smoking be considered a pandemic? Is it because it is not contagious? But we have scientifically known for a rock-solid three decades or more that smoking is deadly, and yet, in about fifty-five countries, at least one-fifth of all deaths in males are attributable to smoking. These countries generally are high- or very high-life-expectancy countries, mostly located in Europe (thirty-three countries).

You can pass off the same arguments or justifications on this. From a very basic viewpoint, we know that eight million deaths will occur from smoking. Isn't that flooding and overwhelming our health systems? Or are our health systems expecting that and built for it?

It wasn't long ago that the majority believed that smoking did not cause disease and was socially and culturally acceptable. Doctors agreed by giving their endorsements.

It was almost like if you were not smoking, you were an outsider—anti-social. It was safe and effective to help people remain calm and relaxed. Take a smoke break and feel the outdoors. That was science speaking.

Knowing what is obvious today, is there any parallel we can discern between the tobacco industry and the pharmaceutical industry with their drug products and vaccines? Why wouldn't this be a classic case study for what the pharmaceutical industry is doing now?

Well, from the 1950s onwards, it has been a multi-trillion-dollar industry created by tobacco giants. And in the end, it was wrong.

We, the science, didn't know. Today it is wrong. It was so well controlled and still is today. How did they pull it off? Was it that they had an overwhelming team of lawyers that stunned the system asking them to go ahead and prove it. Tobacco companies were very open about it "Show us the science." Was it the amount of money they spent on lobbying? Or the advertising making it culturally and socially cool to smoke, perhaps? Was it advised by your doctor who told you that there was no scientific evidence or studies suggesting that smoking caused disease, was carcinogenic or filled with toxins? Did doctors ever suggest one brand over another?

Fast-forward to today, and people are still smoking. How is that possible when the science is in? How is this being perpetuated? Oh, you say it's still a personal choice and if people want to smoke that's their business and that the government gets tax revenue. And you accept that? Well, what about the huge health problems created by second-hand smoke? Just under a million people (many of which children) died in the US from second-hand smoke.

What is the reason this is not a pandemic? Every ad on TV promoted why their brand was important to you. The Marlboro Man, Export A, Benson & Hedges.

Tobacco argued that banning the sale of a product was against their rights.

The scientific method used in the political arena is science, and a medical claim is treated as though it is false until it's proven beyond a reasonable doubt. But in politics, a medical claim may be accepted until proven false or harmful beyond a reasonable doubt. It is a basic principle of the scientific method that the burden of proof belongs to the proponent of a claim.

Advertising Today

For fifty years, the science told us that smoking is safe and effective. And obviously, this continues today, albeit in other contexts.

If you repeat a lie often enough—that smoking is sexy, healthy, and "cool"—lots of people will believe it. The main trick was to get them hooked while they were young.

One of the biggest myths at the time was advertising that certain brands were safer. Safer than what? Fresh air?

Smoking Camels could give them "healthy nerves," "a flow of energy," "relief of fatigue," and "better digestion."

Smoking a pack of cigarettes means two hundred inhalations of carbon monoxide, cyanide, and arsenic. Madness. But it is still okay today.

This was the science. The public was told that "More Doctors Smoke Camels Than Any Other Cigarette." The public was told that "Many Leading Nose and Throat Specialists Suggest... Change to Philip Morris." The public was told that "20,769 Physicians Say Luckies Are Less Irritating" and that "According to 19,293 Dentists, Viceroys Can Never Stain Your Teeth!" Some ads even appeared in medical journals.

Oh, we could say, that was in the 60s, 70s, and 80s. The science was not known but that is BS. Really. Then what about the 90s and right up to now? What has changed? It is really hard to compare with the Covid vaccines because the vaccines are experimental. Yet we have been given a narrative that Covid is safe and effective

How many doctors and medical officials today would even think that smoking is not terrible for your health? Why, then, hasn't the government moved faster to stop this epidemic?

The tobacco industry outmaneuvered any control by coming up with all sorts of "scientific breakthroughs—above all else, the filter. Manufacturers began promoting "health protection." At least one filter was made partly out of asbestos.

The government did step in has stepped in with power. No more advertising and warnings on cigarette packages. No smoking rules everywhere.

Consumer Psychology

If you were buying a car, many factors might influence your selection. But if it didn't run, you wouldn't want it. With patent medicines, however, consumer satisfaction doesn't necessarily require the presence of effective ingredients. There are two reasons for this. The first is that most illnesses are self-limiting.

The second is a matter of psychology. When people feel better after taking a medication, they tend to think that the medication has helped them. But to really determine whether a medication is effective, it is necessary to know whether improvement would happen just the same without it. This accounts for the many who celebrated their Covid doses as euphoric and liberating. Obviously, they were really only personally saved from the media hype. They can still get covid and transmit. And for all of those, mainstream delivering the narrative did their job.

Scientists can test this by comparing treated and untreated ("control") groups. However, evaluations of drug effectiveness must also take into account the "placebo effect", whereby people feel better simply because they think they are being helped.

The placebo effect can be both powerful and misleading. The pill peddlers know that about forty out of every one hundred people will notice an improvement in their headache even if given a sugar pill!

Confidence in a remedy can enhance its placebo effect. We've seen this with so many people on social media after getting the jab—how uplifting it was, the feeling of euphoria, no fear, and one big step to normalcy. The patent drug industry knows this and tries hard to build up your faith in its products.

Drug-makers take advantage of people's desire to control their own destiny by "doing something" instead of letting nature run its course.

Public faith in patent medicines is enhanced by widespread beliefs that products must be effective in order to be marketed and that health advertisements must be truthful "or else they wouldn't be allowed." But the patent drug industry has generally stayed one step ahead of the law. The U.S. Federal Trade Commission had to struggle for sixteen years to get the word liver removed from Carter's Little Liver Pills because the pill had nothing to do with the liver.

Protect yourself if you use non-prescription medicines. You owe it to yourself to do so in a scientific and responsible manner. Take the time to inform yourself.

Calls For Banning Direct-To-Consumer Drug Ads

There have periodically been calls for the FDA to severely curtail or ban direct-to-consumer advertising. However, free speech arguments regarding the right of a manufacturer to market its products, for the most part, prevent this.

In a series of cases dating back to the 1970s, the courts ruled that product advertisements were a form of "commercial speech." Banning or restricting commercial advertising therefore violates the First Amendment protections of freedom of speech.

The NCBI (National Center for Biotechnology Information) understands that pharma ads misinform patients. By promoting a drug as the solution to a health problem, these advertisements may lead viewers to believe that adopting healthy behaviors, such as a good diet and exercise, are ineffective or unnecessary. And it is working.

Because consumer advertising rarely focuses on public health messages about diet, exercise, addictions, social issues, and other treatments, it can also cause people to falsely believe that they are well-informed, reducing their motivation to search for more reliable information.

This is particularly true for "first-in-class" drugs. Clinical trials required for FDA approval typically aren't designed to detect rare adverse effects, and current methods of post-marketing surveillance often fail to connect adverse events that have a high rate of background prevalence with the use of a particular drug.

Drugs that are expected to be "blockbuster" sellers are also most heavily promoted early in the product's life cycle, which can present a public health risk because the drug's safety profile is not fully known at that point.

The safety problems with the prescription medication for arthritis symptoms was Vioxx from Merck, is perhaps the most frequently cited example regarding this issue.

Vioxx was among the most heavily promoted drugs in the US from 1999 to 2004. During that time, Merck spent over $100 million per year to build the drug into a blockbuster seller, with annual sales of more than $1 billion in the US.

Patients requesting it thought that they were advocating for themselves by asking for a drug that they thought was better than its competitors, not knowing that it could lead to stroke or myocardial infarction. Approximately 88,000 Americans had heart attacks, and 38,000 of them died along with 5B payout from thousands of lawsuits. On September 30, 2004, Merck voluntarily withdrew Vioxx from the market.

Other drugs that were heavily promoted to consumers have also been linked to safety advisories and FDA black-box warnings. A black box warning is the FDA's most stringent warning for drugs and medical devices on the market. Black box warnings, or boxed warnings, alert the public and healthcare providers to serious side effects, such as injury or death.

Wow. The IOM (Institute of Medicine) recommended that a special symbol appears on the packaging for the first two years that a new drug is on the market. And how does that help the consumer?

In response to the Vioxx recall, PhRMA also issued guidelines recommending that the new drug DTCPA be delayed until the drug's safety profile is fully established and health care professionals are educated as to the drug's proper use.

The common theme here is comparable to vaccines. It is based on the ability to leverage a proven benefit to all of humankind. The success of disease-fighting biologics in vaccines became an opportunity to fight all diseases. What was needed was undisputable faith in vaccines that they could protect against disease. And the market is wide open for the hundreds of diseases that are just floating out there, waiting for an outbreak. And if not? Create one! But what would implode this trillion-dollar opportunity? After all, billions had been spent on lobbying, and tight connections with the CDC, FDA there. And talk about immunity. Immunity to prosecution: that was a lock-in 1986. Any hint that vaccines could cause harm would be devastating. It would be hard to cover up unless there was a plan.

In Sad Summation

How is it that the tobacco industry is allowed to carry on? In Canada, there are 5.5 million smokers with forty-five thousand smoking-related deaths each year. Covid deaths in comparison are 26k deaths of direct and related death with assumed Covid. Smoking causes one in five of all deaths and costs $6.5 billion in healthcare each year. The US has over five hundred thousand deaths each year, and healthcare costs are $170 billion.

So, is it the tax revenue from tobacco going to the government that keeps them going? Is it lobbying to protect their rights to make a product? Or is it that the key beneficiary here is the pharmaceutical companies? There are hundreds of prescription drugs, medical devices, and operations for tobacco related cases.

Explain how Covid 19 is the only crisis that needs an advertising campaign paired with a constant barrage of repetitive narrative propaganda on the TV and in the streets.

Why hasn't tobacco been abolished?

Explain, if all the vulnerable people have already been vaccinated, why do all the healthy people need to get vaccinated if you're already protected by your own vaccine and the recovery rate was already 99.96% without the vaccine.

3
The Erosion of Trust

"I think the entire pharmaceutical industry has a lot of work to do to restore public trust."

—Kenneth C. Frasier

- Biggest Defrauders Of Government
- Billion Dollar Payouts
- Advocate For Your Health

Chapter 3

George Merck, the founder of the third-largest pharmaceutical company, stated the following in 1950:

> *"We try never to forget that medicine is for the people. It is not for the profits. The profits follow, and if we have remembered that, they have never failed to appear. The better we remember it, the larger they have been."*

Big Pharma is the nickname given to the world's pharmaceutical industry. Big is an understatement. Revenues include Johnson & Johnson at $85 billion, Merck at $45 billion, and all in the Top 10 at $35 billion-plus. Each of these companies had leading vaccine outfits.

Who owns Big Pharma or who does Big Pharma own? Pharma is a business and is controlled by its shareholders, who are invested to make a profit. So, yes, pharma is driven by money. Pharma has regulatory capture meaning they have more than just influence on any and all regulations that govern them. That has made them very powerful. The Pandemic has created a new awareness for everyone on how we trust the pharmaceutical companies, their drugs, their vaccines, the CDC, FDA, and more with a less than remarkable track record that few people know about.

It is not to say that the advances in medical science have enriched and saved so many lives. These medical advances have come in the form of ever-increasing medical knowledge, medical breakthroughs, diagnostic abilities, surgeries, and treatment options. Medicine in its social role is responsible for health promotion and ill-health prevention.

Simply put, we all know, understand, want, and need the best healthcare possible. We need and expect to be able to trust the industry to provide safe products. The science needs trust. We believe, we trust, and we expect our doctors to provide their knowledge and guidance for healthcare. Pharma, however, has been pushing those boundaries.

Since the shock of the pandemic, there has been a global awakening about our health, our immune system, science, misinformation, the flip-flops, hypocrisy becoming the new normal, political leaders trying to get it right, and much more. We have seen how quickly our lives can and have changed with our freedom of rights taken away.

Is now the time to look at what you think and believe about medicine, vaccines, treatments, freedom, and censorship? There is a lot at stake here. Is it not worthwhile to take the time to understand what medicine or vaccine is going into your body or your child's body? More importantly to have the choice. How much time do people take to look at what is a healthy diet? Quite a lot I would think, but understanding and reviewing the food labels although there are no major issues regarding accuracy there. Regardless, they probably take a lot more time pondering calories than researching medicine and/or vaccines.

There is certainly an understanding here that you don't intend to know more than the pharmacist or doctor. It also really shouldn't put you in a position of mistrust of either. The prescription insert at least equips you with the science behind the medication on instructions and potential symptoms. The same with a vaccine insert—except you don't get to see that one and for good reason. There is no informed consent with the Covid vaccine. You get the jab then you get an info sheet of potential reactions. It should be the other way around. So, there is a starting point to do some research on specific studies from the Institute of Medicine, FDA, Health Canada, and more. It's a starting point for questions and important dialogue with your doctor.

If you think about buying a new or used car from a certain dealer, you might check what recalls have occurred. Some look to online reviews and may be swayed by a specific dealer whose level of service isn't up to par. It wouldn't take much for one to move elsewhere. Even if the issues were just about employees, their track record is there. The same applies to restaurants. You can do the same with the Pharma companies' medications and vaccines. But who does that? There is always information about certain drugs or vaccines and their success and adverse events. Except, in this case, we don't. Who checks the track record of a prescription drug your trusted doctor recommends? What if there were issues being reported but in the world of pharma this takes a year to several years before lawsuits come into play. Yet the negative reports were adding up and being not reported by the media. The drugs Vioxx for arthritis and Johnson & Johnson talcum powder come to mind.

The global revenue for pharmaceutical companies is approx. $1.2 trillion. By 2024 it is expected to be $1.7 trillion. A significant jump. Between 2015 and 2019, American companies introduced a total of 120 new chemical or biological substances. Within the same period, Europe introduced nearly sixty new entities.

The pharmaceutical companies tell us that they turn high prices of products into research toward new cures for diseases. It's true that, at least in the US, they seem to be picking up most of the research tab for the rest of the world. The question is, how do they define "research?" At any rate, if we're curing diseases, maybe it's worth it.

They've also spent billions on fines, settlements, and jury verdicts. Not all by mistakes but often by knowing that a drug/vaccine creates adverse reactions and death but selling it anyway.

How Big Pharma Controls Medical Schools - This Is Good Business!

Doctors themselves are a selective process and we've got doctors that are really smart people today—brilliant medical doctors.

There's a very selective process there. You just don't get into med school unless you've got a pretty good head on your shoulders, but they're not taught a lot about natural cures or dietary cures. They're primarily taught about drugs and drug reactions and the chemistry of this and the chemistry of that.

Many of them have made the transition, and they speak quite openly about it now. The pharmaceutical industry knows that if they give large grants to these universities, they receive a double benefit. First of all, they have the appearance of being philanthropists, which is certainly good for public relations. It is, of course, a great thing to do, but there is the intent to influence these institutions.

Big Pharma is also the biggest defrauder of the Federal Government under the False Claims Act, according to consumer watchdog group Public Citizen. The industry has a history of fraud, bribery, lawsuits, and scandals. Despite criminal charges and fines, Big Pharma companies continue to do business. A necessary evil because of the real need for medicines.

Big Pharma Spending

According to *BMJ,* a British Medical Journal which publishes over fifty of the world's leading medical and allied science journals, for every dollar spent on "basic research," Big Pharma spends $19 on promotions and advertising.

From 1998 to 2016, Big Pharma spent nearly $3.5 billion on lobbying expenses—more than any other industry. Yes, they even beat out tobacco.

Big Pharma contributes heavily to the annual budget of the FDA (U.S. Food and Drug Administration). They contribute about two-thirds of the FDA's budget. The pharmaceutical companies have been allowed to pay the FDA prescription drug user fees[4] to "help" the FDA in the process of approving drugs for the sale and distribution in the U.S. They use their profits and an army of 1,378 paid lobbyists to spread their influence on Capitol Hill.

[4]http://www.pbs.org/wgbh/pages/frontline/shows/prescription/hazard/independent.html

Critics say Big Pharma relies on manipulative tactics to increase sales. They say it uses expensive advertising to sway lawmakers, FDA, and the public.

Ghastly Ghostwriting

The Pharma companies will hire professional writers to write medical journal articles. Then, they will pay doctors to put their names on an article. They are published in well-known journals/ publications. When other doctors are doing their research and review, they effectively end up reading an article getting his info from drug-sponsored journals that are essentially written by the drug companies.

Has your doctor been paid by drug companies? Are they prescribing drugs based on these perks? In the U.S. there are twenty-eight states that have a False Claims Act.

In the US, pharmaceutical and medical device companies are required by law to release details of their payments to a variety of doctors and US teaching hospitals for promotional talks, research, and consulting, among other categories.

In 2019, twelve billion in disclosed payments were made to 1,036,163 doctors and 1,249 teaching hospitals.

There were over seven hundred doctors who were paid more than a million dollars by drug and medical device companies despite often damning scrutiny from prosecutors and academics. Sadly, such high earnings have become commonplace.

More than 2,500 physicians have received at least half a million dollars apiece from drug makers and medical device companies in the past five years alone, a *ProPublica* analysis of payment data shows.

And that doesn't include money for research or royalties from inventions.

There is now a US database containing information about what is paid to physicians for speaking and consulting. It allows everyone to search for their doctors in one place.

In the years since its launch, Dollars for Docs has become an essential tool for patients and has been viewed more than twenty-three million times. But from the very start, we were bedeviled by a simple question.

The next concern was whether or not the drug company payments linked to doctors' drug choices?

First, there is an online tool to find and compare doctors on a variety of data[5].

Second, there is an online tool that now covers every drug and device company, and any blemishes on their record thanks to the Physician Payment Sunshine Act[6]. The law requires all drug and device companies to publicly report their payments[7].

Our analysis gave us the first signs that the drug company payments were linked to prescriptions. Some of the top prescribers of expensive, brand-name drugs had financial relationships with the drugs' makers.

Doctors who received payments from the pharmaceutical industry prescribed drugs differently than their colleagues who didn't. And the more money those doctors received, the more they prescribed the respective drugs.

It again confirms the prevailing wisdom that there is a relationship between payments and brand-name prescribing.

Takeda Pharmaceuticals

With more than $16 billion in revenue in 2016, Takeda Pharmaceutical Company is Japan's largest drug manufacturer and one of the twenty largest pharmaceutical companies in the world.

Chobei Takeda began selling traditional Japanese and Chinese herbal medicines from a small shop in Osaka, Japan in 1781. This was before they began importing western medicines including the anti-malaria drug quinine.

Their origins and philosophy were not based on Germ Theory from Louis Pasteur but Antoine Dechamp's theory on natural healing.

After expanding into seventy countries, they went off their path of more holistic medicine and chose pharmaceuticals. Holistic versus Profit.

[5] https://projects.propublica.org/checkup
[6] https://openpaymentsdata.cms.gov
[7] https://www.propublica. org/article/dollars-to-doctors-physician-disciplinary-records

Takeda's emerging market thrust has been aided by expanding its vaccine divisions—in turn, a blown-away market of $2.9 billion.

The company pushed forward with new growth, but this led to allegations the company was putting profits ahead of patients. One of its drugs, in particular, would result in thousands of lawsuits against the company.

The diabetes drug Actos was one of Takeda's first blockbusters with global sales peaking in 2010 at $4.5 billion. Then, several studies found an increased risk of bladder cancer among patients. By 2012, the company ultimately settled nine thousand lawsuits for a total of $2.4 billion. A jury ordered Takeda Pharmaceuticals[8] and partner d Eli Lilly[9] to pay $9 billion in 2014. Seriously, would you not think at some point earlier the drug safety monitoring and oversight organizations along with the scientists of Takeda should have seen indicators?

Merck Madness

Drugwatch.com reports: Merck paid hundreds of millions in settlements and jury verdicts to thousands of people who say Fosamax (treatment for bone loss) caused their injuries. Multidistrict litigation (MDL) in New York over Dead Jaw Syndrome has mostly been resolved. A second MDL in New Jersey for bone fractures involved more than 560 lawsuits as of May 2018. More Fosamax lawsuits are pending in multicounty litigation (MCL) and state courts.

June 2020 reporting: Merck's Vioxx arthritis drug may have hurt hundreds of thousands of patients, killing a third of them, a senior FDA investigator said at the time.

Dr. David Graham worked at the FDA and in interviews and Congressional testimony criticized his own agency's approval process of the pain reliever. Now he is widely known as a whistle-blower scientist.

Graham described the outcome of Vioxx as "a disaster," one that is "unparalleled in the history of the United States" and that "constituted an unprecedented failure of the nation's system of drug approval and oversight."

[8]https://www.drugwatch.com/manufacturers/takeda/
[9]https://www.drugwatch.com/manufacturers/eli-lilly/

On September 30, 2004, Vioxx was pulled from the market, with roughly two million people worldwide still using the medication.

This for example would suggest Vioxx could be associated with as many as four thousand to seven thousand deaths in Canada?

At the time of its recall, Vioxx had been taken by some four million Americans. Out of those patients who took Vioxx, the arthritis drug may have caused approximately 140,000 heart attacks resulting in an estimated sixty thousand deaths, FDA investigator Graham. These actual numbers here were based on a "model" on other studies from the FDA, and the year Vioxx was introduced, 1999, showed the largest recent rise in American death rates. The year after Vioxx was pulled from the market, American death rates underwent *a substantial and completely unexpected decline.*

Merck paid nearly $7 billion to settle tens of thousands of Vioxx lawsuits[10] and to cover civil and criminal fines. The Doctors who prescribe any medication do their best to keep up on new science, new studies, and most current positive or negative information on drugs. They too have to review and assess so many sources, and unless something is flagged—they prescribe.

From A Vioxx Study

Four heart attacks occur for every thousand patients taking Vioxx.

The newer study was published in the *Canadian Medical Association Journal* (CMAJ) by McGill University Health Centre (MUHC) in May 2006, nearly two years after Vioxx was voluntarily withdrawn by Merck. The results revealed that a quarter of the patients who had heart attacks while taking Vioxx did so within just two weeks of starting the drug, thereby demonstrating that Vioxx-related cardiovascular risks may occur much earlier than previously thought. And more importantly, these should have been early warning signs.

[10]https://www.drugwatch.com/vioxx/lawsuits/

FDA Undergoes Congressional Interrogation

The FDA was also under criticism for what some described as its seemingly cozy relationship with Merck. Well, it's not just cozy with Merck but with all pharma's. Many executives or scientists who work at the CDC, NIH, FDA end up at a pharma company and vice-versa to the point where it has called a revolving door. At a Senate Finance Committee hearing, witnesses described how danger signals of Vioxx went ignored. How is it possible with all the checks and balances in place this could happen with this and so many other drugs? As stated earlier, it is regulatory capture–control of regulations.

Merck Track Record

The Big Pharma Company has also faced patent lawsuits and criminal charges for illegal marketing and price gouging. The federal government and Merck's own shareholders targeted the company's questionable business practices. They accused the company of tax fraud, price gouging, misleading shareholders, and lying under oath.

Patients injured by Merck's drugs have filed thousands of lawsuits against the Big Pharma Company. The drug maker has paid out billions of dollars in damages to patients and their families as a result.

Merck changed Propecia's label in 2011 to warn of the possibility of cancer and sexual side effects. It warned side effects may continue even after stopping treatment. As of May 2018, about 900 Propecia lawsuits[11] remained pending in federal court in New York.

Lessons Learned And Remedies

- Pharmaceutical firms shouldn't run their own studies and then give their feedback to the FDA to get the drug listed.
- Statistical analysis should be done by independent statisticians.
- The FDA should require independence for all phase III studies and most other studies.

[11] https://www.drugwatch.com/propecia/lawsuits/

- When pharmaceutical firms want to do a study, they should contract the study out to independent investigators and not be involved until reporting findings to the FDA.

The Truth Will Prevail

In 1998 the IOM Institute of Medicine published a report "To Err Is to Be Human." It stated that every year, ninety-eight thousand people die in the US due to medical errors. In 2013, the figure was even more astounding, with over two hundred thousand fatalities and those seriously harmed in the millions. Most of these incidents are related to excessive medication and medication-related errors.

Top Big Pharma Lawsuit Verdicts and Settlements:

> These are lump sums dispersed to millions of people. In a twenty-four-year period, Big Pharma companies paid 373 settlements just for marketing fraud. The settlements totaled $35.7 billion.

Public Citizen published this data in 2013. It called its report "Pharmaceutical Industry Settlements: 1991 through 2015."

In 2012, GlaxoSmithKline (GSK) agreed to a $3 billion settlement. It was the largest healthcare fraud settlement in US history. The charges stemmed from certain prescription drugs, including Paxil, Wellbutrin, and Avandia. GSK still ranks in the top ten for its pharmaceutical drug profits.

Johnson & Johnson is the world's largest health care company. It paid $2.2 billion in 2013 for improperly marketing its drug Risperdal. But their profit from this was over $20 billion. Guess it pays off. How many of us know this as we continue to be repeat customers based on doctor's advice. What needs to change?

There have been nearly 20,500 federal talcum powder lawsuits[12] (and many more in state courts) alleging Johnson's Baby Powder and its other talc products led to ovarian cancer. J&J finally removed it from the US and Canada in May 2020. A St. Louis jury awarded $4.69 billion to twenty-two women, and this remains the largest single verdict so far. Is this just the cost of doing business? Is it

[12]https://www.drugwatch.com/talcum-powder/lawsuits

possible at some point over the years that people and their doctors would have recognized this? After all, it was in 1894, the company launched one of its most iconic products: Johnson's Baby Powder, made of crushed talc. Compare it to tobacco or asbestos on the longevity of harmful recognition and looks like talc is the frontrunner.

Companies have paid billions in hip implant lawsuit settlements to people who claim they were injured by metal-on-metal hip implants.

The largest settlement came from DePuy, a Johnson & Johnson company. The implant maker paid about $4 billion to settle eight thousand ASR hip claims in 2013.

Where does it stop? Approximately ten million people misused prescription opioids, 808,000 people misused heroin, and two million people met the criteria for an opioid disorder in 2018. In that same timeframe, 46 800 people died of an opioid overdose. In the medical framework of all their statistics on this, why wasn't there a major intervention? Is it because it takes tremendous amounts of time and resources to mount an inquiry and then to provide evidence-based reasons to halt the basically free prescriptions to anyone? Was it because Big Pharma has influence, power, and lobbying strength to push their agenda stretching it out to the max?

The largest settlement came from DePuy, a Johnson & Johnson company. The implant maker paid about $4 billion to settle eight thousand ASR hip claims in 2013.

Bayer

In August 2020, Bayer agreed to pay $1.6 billion to resolve about 90% of thirty-nine thousand Essure birth control claims[13].

Pfizer and Eli Lilly were sued over false claims and healthcare fraud in the marketing of pharmaceutical drugs. When these companies have billions of dollars at risk, how is it possible they and all other pharmas will be honest? These are just a few of the many unknown, unrecognized stories to the mainstream consumer. Do you think CNN whose revenue is supposedly 70% supported by Pharma going to give

[13]https://www.drugwatch.com/essure/lawsuits

any details that may frown upon Pharma? Not going to happen. Almost every ad on CNN is pharma-related.

In 2019, several social media firms pledged to act against the anti-vaccine movement. Facebook announced that it would not recommend content that contained misinformation on vaccines. YouTube removed advertisements from anti-vaccine videos, meaning the account holders would not make money, and Twitter ensured that the National Health Service or Department of Health and Human Services would appear as the first result for anyone searching for vaccine-related topics in the UK and USA, respectively.

Pharma Lawsuits

A survey of corporate counsel finds that US companies face a staggering average of 305 lawsuits at any given time. It also notes that government inquiries—particularly from the Securities and Exchange Commission and the Occupational Safety & Health Administration—and internal investigations requiring outside counsel are on the rise.

Big Pharma is one of the most powerful industries in the world. The global revenue for pharmaceuticals was over $1 trillion in 2014. But nowhere else in the world do the drug and medical device industries have as much power and make as much money as in the US.

Six of the top ten pharmaceutical companies for 2017 have their headquarters in the US. These include Johnson & Johnson, Pfizer, Merck, Gilead, Amgen, and AbbVie.

But only 28% of Americans have a good opinion of Big Pharma. In fact, Big Pharma is the second most hated industry in America. It's right in the mix with the tobacco industry and the oil, gas, and chemical industry.

The Pfizer Meningitis Trial

In 1996, US pharmaceutical manufacturer Pfizer conducted a trial of the meningitis drug Trovan (trovafloxacin) on two hundred children at the state-run Infectious Diseases Hospital (IDH) in Kano, Nigeria.

At the time, a triple epidemic of meningitis, measles, and cholera in the city had killed around twelve thousand people. One hundred children were put on Trovan and one hundred on the antibiotic ceftriaxone. Eleven children participating in the trial died, and others suffered paralysis, brain damage, and slurred speech. Pfizer claimed it was meningitis that had made the affected children sick. The families alleged the clinical trial was improperly conducted and lacked parental consent.

In 2003, Kano State filed a $2.75 billion lawsuit against Pfizer, which ended in an out-of-court settlement in 2005. Several of the children involved have also been compensated. For anti-polio campaigners, the case gives "practical evidence that there is harm in the polio vaccine, just like Trovan, with which they convinced parents," said Abdullahi Musa, a Kano-based pediatrician.

"The Pfizer drug trial was a real setback against not only polio vaccination but to other child health interventions in the north because it destroyed public confidence and made the anti-polio campaign readily believable," said polio vaccinator Abdulhamid Barau.

This article was produced by IRIN News while it was part of the United Nations Office for the Coordination of Humanitarian Affairs.

Trust—A Perspective

"I can't understand how the West will spend millions of dollars in providing medication against polio for our children while they systematically killed thousands of Muslim children in Iraq and Iran by imposing an embargo that denied them access to basic medicines, making them scarce. Then expect me to believe that you want to save my child from polio for free."

How could I be so naive as to allow my children to be given polio drops by people who go door-to-door giving the vaccine free while the government has failed to provide medication for the most urgent diseases affecting us, such as malaria and typhoid?

Most people understand polio is caused by a virus, but even so, there are fears the vaccine could be harmful. Nobody wants their child to be crippled by polio, and nobody wants her child to be sterile, either.

In 2003, to address these concerns, the Kano State government (in Nigeria) and the federal government set up committees of doctors and clerics to test the polio vaccine. Following trials in Nigeria, South Africa, and Indonesia, they declared the vaccine safe.

However, they also confirmed the presence of traces of two sex hormones—estrogen and progesterone—that are used in contraceptive medicine, which reinforced the sterility rumors in some communities.

There are so many articles that only go far as to say that vaccines are safe and effective. Very few have delved down into the minds of these so-called vaccine radicals to ask what it is about vaccines is their issue.

Physicians, just like our police, ambulance drivers and more... we want them to be there when we need them. Physicians, as part of the system, have been trained to think a certain way. And when they're in that system, it is presumed to be the best. What alternative(s) could care or health providers know?

There is so much information out there. Parents want to be heard, but the media doesn't pick up any of their stories. Doctors don't have the time to look into it.

Is Sick The New Normal?

With many consumer foods, pharmaceuticals, specialized medicines, and vaccines, we rely heavily on the belief that "if the ingredients weren't safe, 'they' wouldn't be available to you and me. Our government has standards."

It is your responsibility to do research, ask questions, and learn about what goes into your body. You are free to eat what you want, smoke what you want and you should be free to decide which (if any) medicinal or biologicals to ingest. The same freedom should apply to an experimental treatment. The massive media dialogue and campaigns all cater to get your vax and all our communities will be better.

The CDC schedule was created as fair guidance. It was approved, but there were no studies undertaken that show it's a safe schedule. In a Journal of Pediatrics survey of US parents with children between the ages of six months and six years old reveals that about 13% of parents used a vaccination plan that varied from the Centers for Disease Control and Prevention-recommended schedule because of concerns that receiving multiple vaccinations in a short span of time is less safe than delaying certain vaccines.

The Supreme Court in the US stated that vaccines are unavoidably unsafe and that there shall be no more lawsuits regarding children injured or killed by a vaccine. No one can be held accountable other than the parent.

US Congressman Bill Posey describes how he believes every member of Congress should cosponsor studies to make sure the vaccines we give our children are safe. The system has been set up in a way that bars us from the truth, and that is a profound policy problem. People are just going to sit around be politically correct and not worry about it.

Back in 2018, ICAN(Informed Consent Action Network, through its attorneys, submitted an FOIA request for all communications exchanged between Dr. Frank DeStefano, Director of the CDC's Immunization Safety Office, and the pharmaceutical companies GSK, Sanofi, and Merck, which make and sell most vaccines for children.

The CDC located responsive documents but withheld a substantial amount in its production, claiming a "deliberative process" privilege.

In other words, the CDC was claiming that the communications between these for-profit pharmaceutical companies and the director of CDC's immunization safety office were not going to be released because they involved discussions setting CDC policies or decisions!

More than two years later, and only after a lawsuit was filed, the CDC withdrew its objection when ICAN forced it to defend this preposterous position in open court.

In 1986, when all vaccine manufacturers were granted immunity from liability (the only product in American to be granted such a pass), Congress made HHS (Health and Human Services) and its agencies responsible for vaccine safety. The CDC's Immunization Safety Office is supposed to play a central role in ensuring the safety of these liability-free products.

As you know, the CDC vigorously promotes the administration of the approximately seventy-four doses of vaccines on its childhood vaccine schedule, most of which are made and sold by GSK, Sanofi, and Merck.

What we do not know is whether the CDC takes its role as a watchdog over the pharmaceutical companies seriously, especially when those companies earn billions of dollars selling these vaccines.

In order to find out whether the Director of the Immunization Safety Office, Dr. Frank DeStefano, has been fulfilling his responsibilities as a watchdog, ICAN submitted an FOIA request to the CDC.

The request sought all of DeStefano's communications with GSK, Sanofi, and Merck while he was the Director of the Immunization Safety Office.

The CDC located 281 pages of responsive records, of which eighty-one pages were completely withheld and thirty pages were redacted. The CDC explained it was withholding the eighty-one pages because:

After a careful review of these pages, some information was withheld from release pursuant to 5 U.S.C. §552 Exemption 5. (Exemption 5 protects inter-agency or intra-agency memorandums.) Information withheld under this exemption was protected under the deliberative process privilege.

The deliberative process privilege protects the decision-making process of government agencies.

The deliberative process privilege protects materials that are both pre-decisional and deliberative.

Dec 29, 2020, From ICAN

The Informed Consent Action Network ("ICAN") is a non-profit organization that advocates for informed consent and disseminates information necessary for the same with regard to all medical interventions.

Indeed, the importance of capturing all potential health issues for a material duration during a clinical trial is reflected in the trials of, for example, the drugs Enbrel, Lipitor, and Botox, which had safety review periods of 6.6 years, 4.8 years, and fifty-one weeks respectively, each with a placebo control group. As another example, the weight-loss drug Belviq, indicated only for adult use, was safety tested in a placebo-controlled trial for two years before being licensed by the FDA.

Through its attorneys, they demanded that the Centers for Disease Control & Prevention (CDC) produce "documentation sufficient to reflect any case(s) of transmission of Hepatitis B in an elementary, middle, or high school setting." After a search of its records, CDC conceded that "A search of our records failed to reveal any documents pertaining to your request." Meaning, the CDC could not find documentation of a single case of Hepatitis B being transmitted in a school setting. The CDC admits it has no proof and only did a five-day study. Seriously? Perhaps this is a questionable vaccine right after birth?

This is not the only vaccine that did a bogus study. But wait we have heard, we have been told by our Doctors that studies have been done and they are safe and effective all being the gold standard. Well, it's true a study was done making it deceptive narrative, and bet your Doctor does not know either it was 5 days.

Hepatitis B is a disease spread by bodily fluids. It is transmitted mostly through sexual contact or sharing needles, syringes, or other drug-injection paraphernalia. The CDC nonetheless actively encourages this vaccination for all one-day-old babies and also encourages states to mandate that any child that does not receive the Hepatitis B vaccine series to be expelled from school. Exclusion from school is well documented to result in various psychological, developmental, and opportunity harms.

The fact that the CDC actively encourages expelling children from school for not being fully vaccinated with the Hepatitis B vaccine series while not being able to point to one single case of transmission in a school setting reflects that the CDC's real concern is not with the health of children but, rather, with its blind, religious, and unquestionable belief in vaccination. This is also evidenced by the fact that children with Hepatitis B are permitted to attend school yet those who have not been vaccinated but are uninfected are not.

Also alarming, as pointed out in a prior legal update, is that ICAN provided the CDC, FDA, and HHS numerous opportunities over the past three years to provide proof that it licensed the Hepatitis B vaccines based on clinical trials that reviewed safety for more than five days after injection. All they were able to provide was a litany of excuses–not science. In response, ICAN's legal team formally filed a petition to the FDA on September 2, 2020, demanding that the licensure of the Hepatitis B vaccines be revoked or suspended until their safety, as required by law, is determined in a properly designed clinical trial of sufficient duration.

If the CDC does not have documentation to support Hepatitis B being transmitted in a school setting, it should, at least, direct schools to stop excluding students who are not vaccinated for Hepatitis B and, at best, immediately cease encouraging states to require this vaccine to attend school. ICAN will be taking further action in this regard and will keep fighting to bring the truth to light regarding this product.

Vaccine Inserts

Vaccine inserts say 150-plus adverse reactions. Why? Because these are known reactions. The first ones on the list are the basic ones that media doctors describe. Some soreness, redness, itchiness, mild headache, nausea, and more—meaning the vaccine has started to do its work, triggering an immune response.

Does anyone really know about these inserts, discuss with their doctors, and question where to look for studies or reliable sources?

What is the synergistic effect of combining three or four or eight vaccines in one shot? What studies have been done on this? The WHO and partners have already bundled multiple vaccines in one dose. This is cost-effective and reduces the concern of parents taking their children every few months to get 80 plus doses by the time they are 18 years old.

Today, when your child is getting the vaccination, they call this ten or fifteen minutes of discussion with the doctor. That's barely enough time for the doctor to go over informed consent (if it is done at all) and briefly describe the CDC guidance of vaccinations and the diseases you are protected from via the schedule of vaccinations.

The federal government does have to protect the borders, so they can make laws relating to all people coming into the country who have infectious diseases. Fifty states have medical vaccine exemptions.

Forty-seven states account for religious beliefs while vaccine exemptions in sixteen states can pertain to medical issues, religious beliefs, or conscientious matters (which have soared).

However, many of these states are pushing to make vaccines mandatory. Even experimental-use authorization vaccines like those for COVID-19. All exemptions swept away. California was the first to push for thousands of immune-comprised children and adults to be forced to be vaccinated even though the doctor declares the vaccine would be high risk and could cause irreparable harm.

Medical doctors do not learn a lot about vaccinations except for the schedule. Do they know that there's the potential that a certain amount of material in vaccines impairs many cell structures and cell functions? The insert that comes along with the vaccines covers this, but it's largely ignored. In fact, I have never been shown or given one by my doctors.

The American Association of Pediatrics has a section dedicated to teaching Physicians how to persuade parents to accept vaccines, and some refer to older studies—all the way back to 2010—stating that vaccination has no adverse effects on neural psychology outcomes. But the number of doses and the number of vaccines has doubled since then, and studies have not kept up.

Is it possible that some vaccines work and some don't on different people? Is it possible that some vaccines cause severe side effects? Since all vaccines are deemed to be safe and effective, they are painted with the same brush. Vaccines have not been proven that one size fits all.

One child in six in the US is now learning disabled, and the number of Asperger's and autism cases is skyrocketing. One in four hundred develops diabetes, and millions more suffer rheumatoid arthritis and epilepsy. 30% of young adults have been diagnosed with a mental disorder—bipolar, schizophrenia, etc.—and this has coincided perfectly with a tripling of the numbers of vaccines since the 1986 Act to indemnify all vaccines of liability meaning disablement and death.

4 The Quest for Transparency

"It is a capital mistake to theorize before one has data. Insensibly one begins to twist facts to suit theories, instead of theories to suit facts."

—Sir Arthur Conan Doyle

- What The People Want
- Hidden Truths
- Failure Of Vaccine Safety Monitoring

Chapter 4

In a race to save all of us in the world from all diseases, the pharmaceutical companies are full speed ahead researching vaccines. The profit from just one vaccine on the FDA schedule could mean billions. There are 170 new vaccines in various trial stages. The last review on just Sars Cov 2 vaccines is that there are 90 of them in the works getting ready for your bi-annual booster against all the variants. The call to arms from the science, the media, and your government will be a lighter form of narrative because the masses are believed to be well controlled, obedient, and will line up to get the jab to protect you and your community.

There are many groups of people throughout the world with varying opinions about vaccines. The largest group is made up of the thousands of parents who had a baby or young child who was healthy, attentive, active, and responsive; then, their world crashed when the vaccination time came, and then the next day or months later, their child regressed into Autism (Autism Spectrum Disorder) with neurodevelopmental problems. The parents believed it was the vaccine. The Doctor says the vaccine is safe and effective that there is no correlation with causation. The parents and the child's life change drastically forever. The situation most likely will go unreported as a serious adverse event and the doctor will continue to monitor and want the parent to get the next vaccine on the schedule.

Vaxxed Or Unvaxxed

Just like anything else, we want safety, yet the Flint Michigan water disaster did not listen to the anti-contaminated water group. No one listened to the anti-Ford Pintos in 1970 (the most dangerous car ever launched... and launched with full knowledge of the risks its fuel tank carried).

It took decades for those of the anti-tobacco movement to finally get tobacco companies to acknowledge that their product causes cancer. And even today Covid dwarfs the number of hospitalizations and deaths due to tobacco.

Everyone knew it, but the narrative was the science. The studies and expert respiratory experts were able to push the narrative that showed no direct link between smoking and any of the long list of lung diseases. There is no direct link! Must have been genetics, air pollution, or toxic environmental issues.

The Anti-Vaxxers

Sounds almost like a terrorist group, and actually, it is portrayed by media as using conspiracies to scare the public.

And just like every situation where there is a safety concern, these individuals, groups, and safety standards groups all the way up to Congress hearings just want to know the truth. Now, the media, Big Pharma, WHO, and other entities have coined the term "anti-vaxxer" for anyone who questions any aspect of vaccinations.

Then, one step further, they minimalize these people as only a few percent of the population. Then, they point to some extreme conspiracies these people are involved in and have (their) news networks repeat the narrative.

Everyone understands the importance of vaccines and the millions of lives saved and their continuance will save even more. But there is no study that can say they are safe and 100% effective. Of course not. That would be an impeccable record.

So, what is the percentage? The misconception leans toward absurd optimism, as the media portrays adverse events as rare—like one in a million.

The vaccination debate has two distinct viewpoints. One is pro-vaccine, and the other is pro-choice. The pro-choice group is called anti-vaxxers by media and the general public who don't know better and that they represent a few percent of the population. Wrong. There is a huge representation of pro-choice people segmented into several different opinions. They include doctors, health care workers, and your neighbor. Some who have seen and experienced, healthier children than those vaccinated. Parents whose children regressed into autism days, weeks or months after a vaccine. Others who believe in natural foods and healing combined with western medication. All groups want the same end result: health.

The pro-vaccine camp chooses to say "listen to the science." The studies, they say, have been done, and vaccines are safe and effective. Yet, this group has never looked at a study or wouldn't even know where to look. And yes, the studies have been done. Several were for 4 days, some 7 days, and other studies have now been exposed for having inaccuracies from whistleblowers.

Those in the pro-choice camp believe that vaccines are important but that the science is corrupt. A top scientist, an epidemiologist from Stanford University John Ioannidis, shocked many scientists with his papers on "Why Most Published Research Findings Are False" There are questions and concerns, but neither Big Pharma nor the CDC wants to have these conversations. Those who are pro-choice know that some areas of science have been compromised for the purpose of financial gain for all parties.

The pro-choice viewpoint is extensive, predicated on religion, a sense of liberty, and the belief that vaccine safety science is flawed (due to known corruption).

Vaccination rights must expand, not detract. Is it ethical for government forces to compel an individual to accept medical procedures that could cause injury or death without free and informed consent, thereby withholding essential rights and privileges? That's what is happening today. Children should not be coerced with ice cream and allowed to make their own decision even without parent knowledge. This is totally unethical by our health advisors and politicians.

There is a growing body of science that points toward the fact that vaccines are leading to a rising number of childhood immune system and neurological disorders.

We should trust our science, our government, and our practitioner. But the trust in vaccines has fractured. Just like the tobacco industry was once safe and effective. But vaccines have a track record of success in saving millions of lives, don't they? Unfortunately, this assertion amounts to damage control that comes in all forms to suppress any investigation or questions regarding the science.

The narrative is that adverse events are always mild—a rash or high fever. That there is no connection with vaccines and the list of Adverse Events in the Autism Spectrum. If that's the case, why list 150 Adverse Events on the vaccine inserts?

And that is the start of the disconnect. The lack of transparency. The inability of an individual to try and start to do some basic research. It takes time and understanding, as it's quite complicated. Now, censorship dismisses all who ask about the truth. There is no greater attempt today at every level to silence any notion that vaccines are not safe and effective.

One of the major requests for studies to be done is one on vaccinated children and unvaccinated children, and it took years for this to be admitted.

One of several doctors who have lost their medical practice has his own results. Dr. Paul Thomas, the author of The Vaccine Safety Plan, worked with parents and patients on informed consent regarding vaccines. Some patients chose not to have vaccinations, some only accept certain ones, and others wanted the schedule spread out. His results at this time will not make published peer-reviewed science journals, but the study showed significant differences. His studies show with his patients over 10 years that unvaccinated children were far healthier than vaccinated children. This is not something that the

FDA, the CDC, WHO, or Bill Gates want to have these results gain any traction. Of course, the media has their back. Dr. Paul Thomas is in legal battles to get his license reinstated.

Under the FOIA Freedom of Information Act: Informed Consent Action Network Legal Team wrote to Health and Human Services.

This letter is in response to your Centers for Disease Control and Prevention and Agency for Toxic Substances and Disease Registry (CDC/ATSDR) Freedom of Information Act (FOIA) request of July 13, 2020, for:

> *"All documents in the CDC's possession which compare the health outcomes between children that have received vaccines and children that have never received any vaccines."*

A search of our records failed to reveal any documents pertaining to your request. In other words, the CDC has not conducted a study of health outcomes in vaccinated vs unvaccinated populations.

Informed Consent: You have to be a self-advocate. What exactly is that, though? Let's take the flu vaccine, for example. Get it at your pharmacy or doctor's office. About 95% of the population believe it is just a shot, has no reactions, is safe and effective, and will protect you. But which shot did you get? Were you advised about the differences? Did you think to ask?

None of these apply and understandably. First, understand, the flu shot is 20 - 30% effective. But the flu shot narrative makes everyone believe they are safe from what it is for. In fact, the narrative of the COVID-19 shot has been portrayed by the media as being just like the flu shot.

Which one of the flu shots did you get? Which one contains mercury? (Sidenote: if the doctor breaks a vial on the office floor, it is considered a lockdown—like, break out the hazmat suits. But it is okay to inject it.) That's the one that has mercury.

Mercury was removed from the majority of vaccines decades ago when there was concern from parents, from groups, from believers that—or perhaps evidence (if not proof)—that there was cause with correlation it was causing serious adverse events. To answer the question, 80% of the global flu shot still contains mercury. And yet people, including pregnant women, line up because they have not researched. and were not given informed consent because they trust their doctor.

2019 WHO meeting discussions actually looked at prenatal as a new market but more research is needed—unless it can off-labeled.

In the US, pharmaceutical companies are liability-free. Canada and nineteen other countries in the world have a "no-fault" Vaccine Injury Compensation program. Meaning: the makers are liability-free.

Canada is the only G7 country that does not have a VIC fund. The only province in Canada that has a "no-fault" VIC program in Quebec, and Ontario has just kick-started such a program.

Perhaps this was a sign that there may be trouble ahead or they viewed what the UK did and pushed out a special government bid for an emergency upgrade to their injury reporting and legal system.

Concerned parents are opting to delay or forgo certain vaccinations for their children for many different reasons.

In Canada, for COVID-19 vaccines, there is fear amongst many people about the adverse effects, as it is a new vaccine and it was made faster than any other vaccine in history. Some will avoid taking the vaccine due to fear of what those adverse effects will be.

If the government attempts to make the vaccine mandatory, it will certainly face legal challenges and hurdles, which may, in fact, result in the opposite of the intended effect, as negative commentary will spread like wildfire over social media. Vaccine Choice Canada is just one group that has lawsuits against the province under Canada's Charter of Rights and Freedoms.

The media, the WHO, and myriad organizations push key reasons to the general public regarding why such vaccines are so important. Weren't diseases already disappearing, people ask, before vaccines were introduced because of better hygiene and sanitation? WHO claims ideas like this are very common in anti-vaccine literature—the intent apparently being to suggest that vaccines are not needed.

This is just not true. Informed Consent people do believe vaccines have prevented diseases and saved lives. Diseases were not disappearing. This is just hearsay. It is, however, true that hygiene, sanitation, clean drinking water, other similar factors have led to overwhelming reductions in disease. WHO even admits this in other writings.

Measles - MMR Vaccine–Measles Mumps Rubella

One example of WHO's nefarious practices is how they've hype measles.

Specific to the US and Canada, they have insisted that there were peaks and valleys throughout the years but the real drop in measles incidence coincided with the use of the measles vaccine beginning in 1963.

So, twenty years prior to the 1963 vaccine, measles was at a high peak, then quickly dropped with herd immunity. The curve had flatlined to very significant lower levels not to be concerned with. By 1960, measles had dropped tenfold before the vaccine was released. Even throughout the 70s and early 80s, when children got the measles, it was a few days off school, some red spots, and a slight fever. And you got natural immunity for life!

Another idea put forth by the WHO: "Can vaccines cause the disease"? Their answer is longwinded and doesn't answer the question. The answer, of course, is yes. Presently, the polio vaccine in Africa is causing more infections than it's preventing. But put in context, it is very rare and the number of cases is said to be low. Another situation is that some vaccines cause shedding or transmission. Meaning six weeks after the shot, the shedding can cause infection in pregnant or immune-comprised individuals.

Why are some vaccines grouped together? WHO describes this as being for practical reasons, citing the fact that they are looking for ways to combine more antigens. This is most concerning for parents, as there is little to no research or studies were done on the impact of three, six, or eight vaccines dosed at one time.

From 1920, deaths decreased steadily before flatlining—from approximately 120 per million in 1920 to approximately two per million in 1960. So, yes, even after a measles vaccine was licensed in 1963. The good news for people who get measles: they develop a natural immunity for life. With the vaccine, studies show that the vaccine wears off and you can choose to get a booster. In cases where the media talks or more like hypes about outbreaks, that they are rare is just false.

In the late 70s, TV sitcoms like *The Brady Bunch* demonstrated how most kids were ecstatic for a few days off school and fun at home when they got the measles. Today, if someone gets measles, it becomes a red flag. A major media alert there has been an outbreak. The rhetoric continues like the sky is falling.

Measles was declared eradicated in the United States in 2002. The CDC shows there has been an average of 320 people in the U.S. each year for the last ten years in the US that get the measles.

This means that one in a million will contract it. Parents do not have informed consent on this. This information is not provided (or even known) by most physicians. Wouldn't this be a reason for many to have vaccine hesitancy?

So, the question is, what purpose do some of the vaccines serve if the diseases have become so much milder? This process of diseases steadily becoming milder is called attenuation and is well known in medicine. We don't take antibiotics or penicillin in case we get sick.

In the 1970s, the DTP (Diphtheria, Tetanus, Pertussis) vaccine received a wave of opposition when it was linked to neurological disorders. This has led to major changes to this vaccine.

Vaccine–The Perfect Product

If the car industry was protected from liability when it came to product defects that caused injury or death, there would be a public uproar. The car industry viewpoint is that people cause accidents. It's like the idea that guns don't kill people, people do. And unless there is enough evidence to prove otherwise, it's all good.

The narrative in the car industry is that "recalls are part of the automotive industry." It doesn't matter what year it is; there are always a few vehicles that need to be recalled due to manufacturing defects. It could be a wiper blade, turn signal, or something equally innocuous. But what about life-threatening problems involving faulty airbags, gas tanks that lead to explosions, doors that collapse on impact, or brakes that don't work? The number of recalls is staggering—like a billion-plus over the last thirty years.

But for vaccines, there is no liability. The consensus is that there are checkpoints—like peer-reviewed studies, the CDC the FDA, the HHS, and many more—that review all the safety studies.

No matter how negligent—no matter how toxic or sloppy—they are when it comes to research (or lack thereof), they can't be harmed. No class-action suit. No downstream litigation costs.

The CDC legacy was called the Public Health Department. It was a quasi-military and vaccine organization initially conceived as a national defense in case of biological attacks on the country warfare from the Russians.

They wanted to be able to deploy a medicine/vaccine to 250 million Americans... with no regulatory requirements because testing would need to be involved. If it was called a "medicine," that would take five years. But if it was called a biologic and made exempt from safety testing (1986), insane profits could be made.

Big Pharma moved quickly, taking control of the CDC, aware that if they lobbied and provided funds, things would run smoothly.

All of a sudden, many vaccines became mandatory—like Hep B, which wasn't even a threat. They mandated them because they could make money.

From three doses in 1960 to 85 doses and more today.

This opportunity was like a gold rush for Big Pharma because now they had a product. They weren't making much money before. Every cost had now been eliminated.

A vaccine can make $60 billion a year for all these companies. The treatments for the fallout are $500 billion a year. The chronic conditions. From Ritalin to inhalers, $600 million epi-pens, and the 50 adverse events that are listed on the manufacturing inserts as side effects.

What Is VAERS?

Vaccine Adverse Events Reporting System (VAERS).

VAERS is an early warning system managed by the CDC and FDA that is designed to find possible vaccine safety issues. Patients, healthcare professionals, vaccine companies, and others can use VAERS to report side effects that occur after a patient receives a vaccine.

Some side effects might be related to vaccination while others might be a coincidence. VAERS helps track unusual or unexpected patterns of reporting that could mean there's a possible vaccine safety issue that needs further evaluation.

VAERS was established in 1990 by the Center for Disease Control (CDC) in the US. It collects reports of problems after vaccination to act as an early warning system in case some of those problems are being caused by vaccines.

A National Immunization Survey (NIS) in 2009 indicated 20% of parents of young children delay or refuse some vaccines, due to a variety of reasons including safety concerns.

The Food and Drug Administration (FDA) has responsibility for assuring the adequacy of evidence supporting the quality, safety, and efficacy of vaccines prior to their licensure as well as for monitoring their safety and effectiveness following licensure.

The FDA, CDC, and Immunization Safety Office (ISO) are supposed to share information and collaborate closely in monitoring and assessing vaccine safety. These activities are primarily carried out using infrastructure such as the Vaccine Adverse Event Reporting System (VAERS) in the US. The results of this data would go a long way to the safety studies, which were supposed to have played an important role in vaccine safety.

Unfortunately, the VAERS system is broken, unlike the car industry where every detail of car safety and accidents are statistically gathered. The organizations that set it up did very little to create awareness in medical offices, institutions, hospitals, and clinics. It was even lesser-known to the general public, who can report any vaccine reaction.

Approximately 1% of adverse reactions have been reported as estimated by the CDC. You would have to believe that with the amount of awareness about vaccines in general and more to Covid that VAERS would have an uptick of reporting. Since Covid and now with the vaccine distribution the VAERS reporting system is blowing up with reports of deaths and serious adverse events. But the point here is that the CDC's own statistics paint an unrealistic picture of what the true numbers are. In fact, this is misinforming the clinicians, hospitals, and doctors, who are led to believe that reactions are rare.

Not until the rollout of the COVID-19 vaccine has this been brought to light. Adverse events were rarely reported to the Vaccine Safety Datalink (VSD) and the Clinical Immunization Safety Assessment (CISA) Network.

With rare exceptions, most individual case reports of vaccine adverse events cannot be definitely ascribed to vaccines, nor can a vaccine be definitively ruled out as the cause. The simple finding that an event occurred after vaccination is not sufficient to indicate a "cause and effect" relationship. Parents and patients will not always agree with this reasoning, underscoring the importance of frontline vaccine providers both knowing the basic aspects of vaccine safety science and having strong communication and empathy skills.

Epidemiological studies that show elevated risks of events in vaccinated compared with unvaccinated individuals, especially if the data indicate a specific period of risk following vaccination or a biologically plausible association; provide relatively strong evidence of causality.

The COVID-19 Context

Many reports coming in to VAERS after their vaccination indicate that people dying and others are experiencing significant adverse reactions after getting the vaccine. But here is how *Fact Checkers* takes it out of context, stating:

What Was Claimed from *Fact Checkers*:

Covid-19 vaccines are killing many people according to data on the VAERS system.

Fact Checkers: Our Verdict

Incorrect. Reports on VAERS are not evidence that the vaccine caused these deaths. Data collected so far suggests that Covid vaccines are safe.

So... case closed right? What? Fact-checkers are great. This is not what the VAERS data means. It is a list of reported incidents that took place after vaccination, not necessarily because of it.

Everywhere that the COVID-19 vaccination comes up, you read or hear comments like this: "These vaccines have had incredible safety profiles in the trials and post-authorization. So far, there has been nothing to confirm these awful events," said Dr. John Brownstein, an epidemiologist at Boston Children's Hospital and an ABC News contributor.

Hey, John: everyone knows that the vaccines have skipped many of the safety profiles such as long-term testing, testing for those over the age of sixty-five, testing on animals, and more. That's what is incredible! Then, the move to "Emergency Use" application and acceptance by the FDA allowed other safety audits and protocols to be circumvented.

Then to add another layer of a miscellaneous fact: An average of eight thousand people die each day in the United States. Some of them may have just received a coronavirus vaccine. Really? Case Closed? Vaccines are safe and effective?

"VAERS does not determine death, period," said one spokesperson for the Centers for Disease Control and Prevention. "Just because somebody reports death doesn't mean that the vaccine caused the death. So, we don't use VAERS to determine death rates or anything concerning death."

Reports through VAERS do not necessarily mean that a vaccine caused the adverse event, as anyone can submit reports, regardless of whether an immunization is thought to have contributed. When deaths following receipt of a vaccine are reported, the CDC and Food and Drug Administration physicians review those cases—and so far with the COVID-19 vaccines, there has been no link with immunization.

Moreover, experts said it's not surprising that more death reports would be submitted to VAERS after COVID-19 immunizations compared to the flu, given the increased attention on the vaccine. The narrative here is totally absurd. Increased attention! But these are our experts. Yes, the whole world now know about Covid vaccines!

"The difference in deaths reported following COVID-19 vaccine and flu vaccine administration is likely due to the enhanced reporting of all events occurring after COVID vaccination compared to after influenza vaccination," Dr. Robert Legare Atmar, an infectious disease specialist at Baylor College of Medicine who also evaluates vaccines, said.

In the case of COVID-19 vaccines, VAERS is just one of several vaccine safety-monitoring systems the government has in place to ensure the safety of the vaccine as it's rolled out to a wider population.

But VAERS data isn't meant to allow safety comparisons between vaccines or to arrive at any sort of estimate of a person's chances of dying following an immunization.

Unfortunately, the failings of VAERS are "kept from the consciousness" not only of the public, but also from the doctors, pediatricians, and nurses that the public relies on to provide reliable information as to the safety of vaccines. It is purely a voluntary reporting system which gets little to no recognition, doctors who do know don't report because of the belief the vaccine did not cause the event.

I say "kept from the consciousness" rather than "kept secret" because while these failings are publicly disclosed for all the world to see, they are for all intents and purposes *buried* in documents seldom searched out by the average member of the medical community, much less by the average individual. There are Heads of Hospitals who simply don't know what it is.

You could say that the information has been very effectively hidden in plain sight. The vast underreporting of vaccines' adverse effects has led to dangerous false security when it comes to vaccine safety and an erroneous assumption that the benefits of vaccination far outweigh the risks.

The CDC, the FDA, the Institutes of Medicine (IOM), and Congress to name a few are aware the vaccine monitoring systems are broken and that they still only show a fraction of serious adverse events.

This is what the CDC says about the VAERS system:

> Passive surveillance systems (e.g., VAERS) are subject to multiple limitations, including underreporting, reporting of temporal associations or unconfirmed diagnoses, and lack of denominator data and unbiased comparison groups.
> Because of these limitations, determining causal associations between vaccines and adverse events from VAERS reports is usually not possible.

In 2000, the 6th Report by the Committee on Government Reform addressed the failings of VAERS in its address of the Vaccine Injury Compensation Program. The report states:

Assessment is complicated by the administration of multiple vaccines at the same time, following currently recommended vaccine schedules, because there may be no conclusive way to determine which vaccine or combination of vaccines caused the specific adverse event.

The same Congressional report reads: "Former FDA commissioner David A. Kessler has estimated that VAERS reports currently represent only a fraction of the serious adverse events."

The report continues by noting that the "IOM warned that 'if research capacity and accomplishments are not improved, future reviews of vaccine safety [will be] similarly handicapped.'" So, whose agenda is it to keep VAERS broken?

The IOM has been telling the CDC for over twenty-three years that they have inadequate information (and none at all in some cases) to advise on the causal relationship between vaccines and adverse events for a majority of adverse events reported. In a 1994 report on vaccines and adverse events the IOM stated:

> The lack of adequate data regarding many of the adverse events under study was of major concern to the committee...Although the committee was not charged with proposing specific research investigations, in the course of its review additional obvious needs for research and surveillance were identified, and those are briefly described here.

In 2011, the IOM conducted another study examining the scientific evidence in studies available for 158 vaccine adverse effects. Again, they concluded that they had inadequate information to come to a decision: "The vast majority of causality conclusions in the report are the evidence was inadequate to accept or reject a causal relationship."

What is to stop industries and government from fabricating the truth and "misaligning information?" The people who work for the Federal government are meant to rely on the Whistleblower Protection Act, which protects federal employees who disclose illegal or improper government activities. But today, the fact is that both government agencies and corporations are increasingly using false allegations of research misconduct to discredit scientists who raise questions about government policies and industry practices.

It seems that the CDC, EPA (Environment Protection Association), and FDA—along with other Federal agencies and universities—all tend to support certain government initiatives, policies, and industry practices, and scientists who publish data supporting the government policies and practices that are economically important end up being freely published in the scientific literature.

On the other hand, if data is generated in research that raises questions, it's invariably suppressed. So, why would an institution like the CDC that has sworn to protect their children's health be engaged in ideology rather than science?

Doctors and pediatricians are trained to believe the CDC is beyond reproach, which is in itself a tragedy. In reality, however, there seems to be a revolving door between the CDC and the vaccine industry—a blatant conflict of interest. Julie Gerberding was the head of the CDC between 2001 and 2008 received a lucrative job as president of one of the top vaccine manufacturers, Merck, with stock options.

Does anyone believe that CDC management isn't being influenced by the very companies they're supposed to be scrutinizing?

Dr. Frank DiStefano, who is the current head of the immunization safety office at the CDC, previously left the CDC, went into industry, and then came back to the CDC. And so, you have this incestuous relationship between the pharmaceutical industry and the CDC. Pharmaceutical companies have a list of vaccines being lobbied to get on the CDC vaccine schedule. So it's important to have good relationships.

And can the CDC be trusted to look at the vaccine safety issues because they have a conflict of interest where they are interested in pushing as many vaccines as possible?

Does The CDC Sell Vaccines?

The CDC mission statement states that one of its purposes is to promote vaccines. As such, the CDC sells just under five billion dollars' worth of vaccines every year itself... and it owns the patent... and they are regulating an industry that they are part of. How disturbing is that?

Does it really seem that the CDC's only role is to ensure there's an uptake of all vaccines that are recommended on the schedule?

So, what about the FDA and all the advisory committees? Because there's a whole process to approve drugs through the FDA (for approval) and the CDC (for recommendation). There's also something called the Federal Advisory Committee Act (FACA). Then, there's the ACIP Committee, which is the CDC's Committee on vaccines for recommendation. On the website, they automatically grant a waiver for the conflict of interest for anybody on the ACIP Committee because they believe the "experts."

Conclusions About Stakeholder Concerns

The committee identified concerns among some parents about the number, frequency, and timing of immunizations in the overall immunization schedule. These concerns were not expressed by clinicians, public health personnel, or policymakers in the committee's review.

(WHY? Because they toe the line!) A doctor can lose their practice and become ostracized.

The childhood immunization schedule is considered one of the most effective and safest public health interventions available to prevent serious disease and death.

Furthermore, the committee's review of the literature did not find high-quality evidence supporting safety concerns about the immunization schedule. (This is because high-quality studies have not been done. Secondly, they did not find evidence because they did not look for any.) Many doctors have modified the schedule and/or agreed to work with parents who do not want any vaccines. They have real data available—especially relating to the health of unvaccinated children compared to those who have followed the recommended schedule.

An effective national vaccine program would require a systematic collection of information on the concerns about vaccine safety. A robust communication and engagement strategy that includes a careful study of safety concerns is needed. Currently, the designs used in most studies of vaccinations do not permit a detailed analysis of the impact of parental concerns on the decision to vaccinate their children.

Conclusions About Scientific Findings

Thus, key elements of the entire schedule—the number, frequency, timing, order, and age at administration of vaccines—have not been systematically examined in research studies.

The second major issue that the committee encountered was uncertainty over whether the scientific literature has addressed all health outcomes and safety concerns. The committee could not tell whether its list was complete or whether a more comprehensive system of surveillance might have been able to identify other outcomes of potential significance to vaccine safety.

Conclusions About Research Methods

Vaccine safety is critically important, but a determination of safety is ultimately a value judgment. The committee did not set a specific numerical target or goal for what should be considered "safe enough."

Instead, based on the literature, the committee made a judgment that failed to link adverse effects to schedule exposures or multiple immunizations, concluding that there is no evidence that the schedule is not safe. There was evidence available, but they sought not to include it and wanted to stay inside the framework of the CDC and not go "outside the box" seeking the practitioners who modified the schedule or did not vaccinate their patients.

The committee acknowledges the evidence that reduced immunization coverage is associated with increases in the incidence of vaccine-preventable disease and found inconsistent and anecdotal evidence to imply that the recommended immunization schedule is not safe. Unfortunately, this naturally would be the result because if they did not collect real evidence.

Moreover, existing adverse event detection systems provide confidence that the existing childhood immunization schedule is safe, and the committee recognizes that the federal government invests considerable resources to ensure vaccine safety. This is the most glaring striking statement of all. The VAERS detection system by their own admission is broken and 90% - 99% underreported—so yes, with all the missing data, it would appear to look somewhat safe.

5 In Pharma We Trust

"There are lies, damned lies, and statistics."

—Mark Twain

- Long List Of Human Experiments
- Drugs & Vaccines: Safe & Effective
- Foundation Of A Lie - Whistleblower

Chapter 5

Common Fraud in the Pharmaceutical Industry Includes:

Unlawful kickbacks
Compounded drug fraud
Illegal drug-switching. Misuse of the $340B drug discount program
Medicaid price fraud
Medicare Fraud
Fraud by Pharmacy Benefit Managers (PBMs)

Clinical trials manipulation/fraud against the Food and Drug Administration (FDA)

Off-label marketing/Food Drug and Cosmetic Act (FDCA) violation

Failure to comply with Current Good Manufacturing Practices (CGMP) requirements

- The ACT1986 - No pharma liability
- Tuskegee & Dengue–Secret vaccine tests
- Vaccine Inserts
- Gardasil
- False studies linking Autism/Whistleblower
- National Vaccine Injury Compensation

The Act 1986

Before 1986, hundreds of injury lawsuits were piling up against vaccine manufacturers for significant adverse events, including what many parents believe was autism. This caused Big Pharma to threaten the government to abandon the manufacturing of major vaccines, thus threatening immunizations for the entire country.

It came down to the pharmaceutical companies stating they couldn't make enough money producing vaccines because they were getting sued, and it went to Congress.

Congress subsequently gave these companies immunity from litigation, and now, without liability from litigation, a gold rush for the pharmaceutical companies began, and they rolled out as many vaccines as possible to market and leverage the global vaccination agenda.

Vaccine makers cannot be held liable for negative side effects that parents believe are the result of their products. To be compensated, parents must go before special no-fault tribunals established by the National Childhood Vaccine Injury Act of 1986. Congress created these "Vaccine Courts" with the participation of pharmaceutical companies as a sort of "societal bargain." The payouts, if won, were paid by tax dollars. The payouts to date are over four billion dollars.

The 1986 Act

In the fifty-seven-page opinion written by Justice Antonin Scalia, the Supreme Court explained that the National Childhood Vaccine Injury Act of 1986 (NCVIA or Act) preempts all design-defect claims against vaccine manufacturers brought by plaintiffs seeking compensation for injury or death caused by a vaccine's side effects.

The court's 6-2 decision reasoned that "a vaccine side effect could always have been avoidable by use of a different vaccine not containing the harmful element." The language of the [NCVIA] thus suggests the design is not subject to question in a tort action. What the statute establishes as a complete defense must be unavoidability (given safe manufacture and warning) with respect to the particular design.

This conclusion is supported by the fact that, although products-liability law establishes three grounds for liability—defective manufacture, inadequate directions or warnings, and defective design—the Act mentions only manufacture and warnings. It thus seems that the Act's failure to mention design-defect liability is "by deliberate choice, not inadvertence."

Justice Scalia's opinion further reflected the belief that "[The Vaccine Act] reflects a sensible choice to leave complex epidemiological judgments about vaccine design to the FDA and the National Vaccine Program rather than juries."

In one major lawsuit that did get to the courts, the family that brought the lawsuit against Wyeth (now Pfizer) argued that their daughter suffered seizures as an infant after her third dose of a diphtheria-tetanus-pertussis, or DTP vaccine in 1992. They also stated that she had a serious developmental delay caused by the DTP vaccine and that a safer alternative had existed but not been made available. Eventually, the vaccine was taken off the market in 1998 and replaced with an upgrade.

Pfizer argued that a Supreme Court ruling in favor of the family would have sparked countless lawsuits, including some claiming links to autism, and threatened the supply of childhood vaccines.

Part of the rationale for the Supreme Court's decision came from the fact that "vaccine manufacturers fund from their sales an informal, efficient compensation program for vaccine injuries. In exchange, they avoid costly tort litigation and the occasional disproportionate jury verdict."

After the ruling, American Academy of Pediatrics (AAP) president O. Marion Burton applauded the Supreme Court's decision in a statement. He noted that the "decision protects children by strengthening our national immunization system and ensuring that vaccines will continue to prevent the spread of infectious diseases in this country." Naturally, this was a major win for pharmaceutical companies too.

The AAP, along with twenty-one other physician and public health organizations submitted amicus briefs supporting Wyeth and noted that a ruling against the manufacturer could "precipitate the same crisis that Congress sought to avert in passing the Vaccine Act: "the very real possibility of vaccine shortages, and, in turn increasing numbers of unimmunized children, and, perhaps, a resurgence of preventable diseases."

Ultimately, this decision could have a significant impact on similar vaccine suits associated with adverse events such as autism. Astra Zeneca senior executive Ruud Dobber stated: " This is a unique situation where we as a company simply cannot take the risk if in four years the vaccine is showing side effects." That they need special indemnification. Who knows what vaccines contribute to chronic disease.

Obama Weighs In

During a recent interview in which he expressed willingness to take a COVID-19 vaccine, former President Barack Obama touched on the historical reasons why some black people might be reluctant to do so. As The Daily Wire reported:

> Regarding why some in the black community might be reticent to take a COVID-19 vaccine, Obama pinpointed the Tuskegee Syphilis Study as a possible reason. The infamous experiment, conducted from 1932 to 1972 by the United States Public Health Service and the Centers for Disease Control and Prevention, deceived black men infected with syphilis into thinking they were being given treatment when in reality, they were simply being used as case studies on the long-term effects of untreated syphilis.
>
> "And I understand, you know, historically, everything dating back all the way to the Tuskegee experiments and so forth, why the African American community would have some skepticism," Obama said. "But the fact of the matter is, is that vaccines are why we don't have polio anymore, and they're the reason why we don't have a whole bunch of kids dying from measles and smallpox and diseases that used to decimate entire populations and communities." What kind of remark and some sort of justification statement is this?

Also, the United States government immorally and unethically—illegally—engaged in research experiments in which more than five thousand uninformed and unconsenting Guatemalan people were intentionally infected with bacteria that caused sexually transmitted diseases. Many have been left untreated to the present day.

Although US President Barack Obama apologized in 2010, and although the US Presidential Commission for the Study of Bioethical Issues found the Guatemalan experiments morally wrong, little if anything has been done to compensate the victims and their families.

Funded by the (NIH) National Institute of Health, agents engaged in a series of immoral and unethical human medical experiments conducted without the participants' informed consent. The study involved at least 5128 vulnerable people, including children, orphans, child and adult prostitutes, Guatemalan Indians, leprosy patients, mental patients, prisoners, and soldiers.

Health officials intentionally infected at least 1308 of these people with syphilis, gonorrhea, and chancroid and conducted serology tests on others. The study originally began in the United States but was moved to Guatemala when researchers were unable to consistently produce gonorrhea infections in prisoners at a Terre Haute, Indiana, prison. The public had no knowledge of the experiments for more than half a century, and even today, little is known about these violations of medical ethics and human rights.

The American public is largely unaware of these experiments and the outrageous treatment of Guatemalans, the reports by the US and Guatemalan commissions, or the victims' lack of reparations, compensation, and access to justice through the courts.

Unequal Justice: Guatemala And Tuskegee

The Tuskegee syphilis experiments, involving recompense for past injustice, are directly relevant to the Guatemalan injustices. In both the Guatemala and the Tuskegee experiments, directed by the same principal investigator, the US government engaged in concededly immoral and unethical actions: conducting nonconsensual human medical experiments, not treating infected victims, and deceiving victims and the public.

What about the US government rollout of the polio vaccine? There is no dispute that millions of Americans received polio vaccines that were contaminated with the virus called Simian Virus 40, or SV-40. There also is no dispute that SV-40 is capable of causing cancer, but there is a major dispute as to how many Americans may have received the contaminated vaccine, with estimates up to one hundred million people. There is also a major dispute as to when the polio vaccine supply got cleaned up. In addition, nobody knows how many people got sick or died because of these contaminated vaccines. Lots of discoveries, lots of unknowns but what about the link to cancer?

The CDC indicated that they don't keep records on things that happened forty or fifty years ago and that they could not be very helpful. That in and of itself raised serious questions. We're not talking about the common cold here. We are talking about polio, the most devastating epidemic of the first half of the twentieth century.

We're talking about tainted vaccines that were given to millions of American children and young adults, and the FDA and CDC need to look a little harder for their records. People were told they were safe and effective.

Dengue

Looking to another similar story, it begins on a stage in Manila in 2016 with the introduction of the Dengvaxia vaccine. Dengue is a mosquito-borne disease.

That shot launched a massive vaccine campaign to inoculate nearly one million schoolchildren with Dengvaxia. The goal was to save thousands of kids' lives and prevent an estimated ten thousand hospitalizations over a five-year period.

But in the end, estimates are that more than one hundred thousand Philippine children received a vaccine that health officials say increased their risk of a severe and sometimes deadly condition.

The company tested it in several large trials, but one US scientist, Dr. Scott Halstead, who had studied dengue for more than fifty years with the US military, saw the vaccine's safety data in the clinical trial and knew right away that there was a problem.

For some children, the vaccine didn't seem to work. In fact, Halstead says, it appeared to be harmful. When those kids caught dengue after being vaccinated, the vaccine appeared to worsen the disease in some instances. Specifically, for children who had never been exposed to dengue, the vaccine seemed to increase the risk of a deadly complication.

The complication is rare, says Halstead. Still, he was so worried about the safety concerns that he wrote at least six editorials for scientific journals. He even made a video to warn the Philippine government about the problem.

"I just think, no, you can't give a vaccine to a perfectly normal, healthy person and then put them at an increased risk for the rest of their lives." This of course is the 'one size fits all' vaccine mentality.

The vaccine manufacturer disagreed with Halstead's interpretation of the study's results. The company wrote a rebuttal, asserting that regulatory agencies had approved Dengvaxia "on the basis of the vaccine's proven protection and acceptable safety profile."

The company also said it would perform additional studies to "further access the safety, efficacy, and effectiveness" of the vaccine.

Despite these concerns, in July 2016, the WHO went ahead and recommended the vaccine for all children ages nine to sixteen.

"Yes, we did. It was what we call a 'conditional recommendation' with the emphasis to minimize potential risks," says Dr. Joachim Hombach, who led WHO's review of the vaccine. "We saw the problems. We also clearly pointed to the data gaps."

WHO recommended that Sanofi do more experiments to better understand the vaccine's safety issues. In its assessment, WHO pointed out that the vaccine "may be ineffective or may theoretically even increase the future risk of [being] hospitalized or severe dengue illness" in people who have never been exposed to dengue—which is about 10% to 20% of Philippine children.

WHO's recommendation came three months after the Philippines launched its mass vaccination campaign in April 2016.

A year and a half later, that campaign came to a screeching halt.

In November 2017, Sanofi published an announcement on its website, saying it had new information about Dengvaxia's safety.

Halstead's fears were confirmed. Sanofi had found evidence that the vaccine increases the risk of hospitalization and cytoplasmic leakage syndrome in children who had no prior exposure to dengue, regardless of age.

"For individuals who have not been previously infected by dengue virus, vaccination should not be recommended," the company wrote.

Panic hit the Philippines. In news reports, parents said that the vaccine contributed to the deaths of ten children. Protests erupted. The Congress of the Philippines launched investigations into the vaccine's purchase and the immunization campaign. And Philippine health officials started performing autopsies on children who died after receiving the vaccine. "In total, the deaths of about six hundred children who received Dengvaxia are under investigation by the Public Attorney's Office," the South China Morning Post reported last month. Investigators have not yet released their results.

Here's the problem with Dengvaxia.

Typically, a vaccine works by triggering the immune system to make antibodies against the virus. These antibodies then fight off the virus during an infection.

But dengue is a tricky virus. Dengue antibodies don't always protect a person. In fact, these antibodies can make an infection worse. The dengue virus actually uses the antibodies to help it spread through the body. So a second infection with dengue—when your blood already has antibodies in it—can actually be worse than the first; a person is at a higher risk of severe complications like plasma leakage syndrome.

In its follow-up study, Sanofi found evidence that Dengvaxia acts like the first infection for a person who has not been previously infected. The body produces antibodies against the vaccine, which have a similar potential for harm.

The increased risk seems small. The vaccine raises the risk of hospitalization after a dengue infection from about 1.1% to 1.6%, the follow-up study from Sanofi found. So out of one million kids in the Philippines, the vaccine would cause about one thousand to be hospitalized over five years, Sanofi estimated. (On the other hand, the vaccine would prevent about twelve thousand hospitalizations for a new dengue infection in children who have had a prior dengue infection during this same time period.)

But in the world of vaccines, that's not an acceptable risk. Risk needs to be exceedingly small to be tolerated. For example, with the measles vaccine, the risk of encephalitis is about one in one million, or a thousand times less than the risk from a measles infection, WHO says.

WHO eventually changed its recommendation. The agency now says the vaccine is safe only for children who have had a prior dengue infection.

By the time Sanofi acknowledged this problem with the vaccine, about eight hundred thousand Philippine children had been vaccinated. The Sanofi study estimated that more than one hundred thousand of them had never been infected with dengue and should not have received the shot, according to WHO's revised recommendation.

Given the concerns by Halstead and the initial unknowns about the vaccine's safety, Philippine parents should have been warned about a potential risk, says Dr. Isabel Rodriguez at the University of California, San Francisco:

> "What bothers me most about this story is risk communication," says Rodriguez, who studies dengue in South America. "There was a lot of uncertainty from the beginning [about the vaccine's safety]. That needed to be communicated explicitly. You need to be honest about what evidence is out there.

Dr. Su-Peing Ng, global medical head of Sanofi Pasteur, says the company followed all World Health Organization guidelines while developing the vaccine and communicated honestly throughout the process. "We've always been very transparent in sharing the results of our research," Ng says. "And I just want to stress that we have full confidence in our vaccine as it's been approved by regulatory agencies in over twenty countries."

In hindsight, Ng says, Sanofi wouldn't have done anything differently with the development of the vaccine: "No, we have been very, very close to the research community, working closely with them over the last twenty years in the effort to find a solution for public health needs."

The Repercussions

In April, the Philippine government indicted fourteen government officials over the deaths of ten children who received the Dengvaxia vaccine. The government said the officials acted with "undue haste" in procuring the vaccine and launching the mass immunization campaign. The Philippine Department of Justice said the campaign started before the clinical trials were finished.

In some instances, children were given the vaccine by untrained health workers and allegedly without a proper physical beforehand. Some children allegedly had preexisting medical conditions that made the immunization dangerous. But these children were still inoculated, the government found.

Six Sanofi officials were also indicted for not properly helping children who had serious reactions to the shot. Sanofi disputes this and other allegations, adding in a written statement to NPR:

> "We strongly disagree with the DOJ's findings made against Sanofi's officials (current and past) and we will vigorously defend them. There is no clinical evidence that any reported fatalities were causally related to vaccination.
> We diligently monitor the safety of people participating in clinical studies. We are also performing pharmacovigilance activities and continuously monitoring the safety profile of the vaccine in a real-world setting, including the Philippines."

Regardless of how these trials turn out, the debacle in the Philippines offers a key lesson for governments and manufacturers when it comes to approving and selling new vaccines: Slow down, says physician and bioethicist Keymanthri Moodley. Mistakes with vaccines can erode the public's trust and have long-term consequences for the health of an entire country.

"When a vaccine goes wrong, it creates fear and anxiety in terms of the public, especially the parents," says Moodley, who directs the Centre for Medical Ethics & Law at Stellenbosch University in South Africa. "That fear can impact negatively on the established immune programs that are actually safe and work very well."

Since the Dengvaxia controversy, the confidence in vaccines among Philippine parents has plummeted from 82% in 2015 to only 21% in 2018, a recent study found. Over that same time span, the proportion of parents who strongly believe vaccines are important has fallen from 93% to 32%. The Philippine government you would think would proceed with caution on other vaccines especially the experimental vaccine for Covid. Quite the opposite as they announced in 2021 that anyone that does not get vaccinated needs to leave the country.

In the US, the approval of the vaccine—to be used in Puerto Rico, the US and the British Virgin Islands, and Guam—comes with an important restriction: doctors must have proof of a prior dengue infection to ensure the vaccine will not pose any risks to the child. That's a safeguard Philippine families never had.

It's not likely that anyone was given informed consent to know the risks before getting the vaccine. To discuss the lengthy list that vaccine companies need to put on the inserts on every vaccine similar to when you get a prescription. They list the mild to serious adverse events and death. So here we are rolling out an experimental vaccine to the world.

Vaccine Inserts

The following adverse reactions include those identified during clinical trials or reported during post-approval use of the M-M-R II (Measles, Mumps, Rubella, Varicella) vaccine or its individual components:

Body as a Whole

Panniculitis; atypical measles; fever; syncope; headache; dizziness; malaise; irritability.

Cardiovascular System

Vasculitis

Digestive System

Pancreatitis; diarrhea; vomiting; parotitis; nausea.

Hematologic and Lymphatic Systems

Thrombocytopenia; purpura; regional lymphadenopathy; leukocytosis.

Immune System

Anaphylaxis, anaphylactoid reactions, angioedema (including peripheral or facial edema), and bronchial spasm.

Musculoskeletal System

Arthritis; arthralgia; myalgia.

Nervous System

Encephalitis; encephalopathy; measles inclusion body encephalitis (MIBE) subacute sclerosing; panencephalitis (SSPE); Guillain-Barré Syndrome (GBS); acute disseminated encephalomyelitis (ADEM); transverse myelitis; febrile convulsions; afebrile convulsions or seizures; ataxia; polyneuritis; polyneuropathy; ocular palsies; paresthesia.

Neurological Respiratory System

Pneumonia; pneumonitis; sore throat; cough; rhinitis.

Skin

Stevens-Johnson syndrome; acute hemorrhagic edema of infancy; Henoch-Schönlein purpura; erythema multiforme; urticaria; rash; measles-like rash; pruritus; injection site reactions (pain, erythema, swelling, and vesiculation).

Special Senses—Ear

Nerve deafness; otitis media.

Special Senses—Eye

Retinitis; optic neuritis; papillitis; conjunctivitis.

Urogenital System

Epididymitis; orchitis.

There is a deceptive narrative that vaccines do not cause adverse events or that they are rare. Sometimes, the problems are admitted—but rationalized. We're told that these unfortunate casualties do happen but overall it is necessary for the greater public good.

There has been an awakening about vaccines with more discussion and information being brought to the surface by the pandemic than ever before. So much that misinformation has swirled while other truths were becoming transparent and both needed to be contained. Has the push to make more vaccines mandatory going to backfire because of this pandemic? Or will enough coercion, our rights and freedom will be eroded through the political and media narrative.

The science on vaccines is far from settled. There is enough alarming evidence in the vaccine research and studies—and ultimately in the children and the people themselves who have had the personal experience of a severe adverse event. This doesn't mean vaccines are not safe and effective. It means that there is another side to it that isn't being discussed, and there are many powerful establishments using combined efforts that have kept it that way. The ask from those that question is transparency and the ability to discuss in an open public forum without getting slammed by Big Tech rules of censorship dictating what is disinformation. There is either a personal, professional, or financial agenda that obviously plays a role.

I'm not a researcher, scientist, or doctor. All I've done is look at all of these compelling facts from a high level. It's possible that a lot of people have just made up their minds and intend to go along with "the science." Do you need all these vaccines? According to some science, you do. To protect yourself and others. But you don't often hear the word "risk," except maybe it is low." Are there some vaccines you just don't need?

What Exactly is in Vaccines?

There's other information on what's in vaccines and it is on the CDC website. It is far too much to document here, but some that get the most attention are Aluminum, mercury, and thimerasols."

It may be an opportunity for anyone to look at the next vaccine that they, their pregnant wife, or their child is lined up to take. The flu shot still contains mercury albeit they call it the friendly kind. The link below directs you to the breakdown of *each substance that is injected into your body.*

Even with this list, there are still other ingredients used in the manufacturing process that show up in the product insert.

Formaldehyde is one that many people have heard of, but it has been argued that the amounts are too small to be concerned about and that they cause no adverse health effects. More importantly, it is found in many areas of the environment as well as building materials and synthetic fabrics. But the studies have all regarded inhaling or ingesting the substance. They had no studies done on injection to children or pregnant women[14].

Thimerosal Content In Some Us Licensed Vaccines

It is understood that this was removed from vaccines after the Environmental Protection Association (EPA) stated the levels were too high:

https://www.vaccinesafety.edu/thi-table.htm

A 2017 study looks at multiple comparatives of methyl and ethyl mercury and their toxic effects:

https://pubmed.ncbi.nlm.nih.gov/27161558/

Environmental factors in the development of autism spectrum disorders are covered here:

https://pubmed.ncbi.nlm.nih.gov/26826339/

Comparing births in 1990 with those in 2001 (followed to age ten), the cumulative incidence of autism rose 600%.

Scientific American wrote a news report in March 2017, including a long list of potential causes of the epidemic increase for autism. Naturally, a small percentage was listed as genetic, and then a long detailed argument was made that it had been underdiagnosed and the spectrum has since widened.

[14]https://www.cdc.gov/vaccines/pubs/pinkbook/downloads/appendices/b/excipient-table-2.pdf

Whistleblower–William Thompson

There are hundreds of articles published in scientific journals both supporting and questioning the safety of vaccines. The CDC, to date, has not been able to identify the cause of autism. If such a study found that there is a link with the autism spectrum disorder, the ramifications would shock the globe. Vaccine hesitancy would skyrocket, pharma's stock would plummet, and there would be other obvious fallout.

In 2014, biologist Dr. Brian Hooker received a call from a senior scientist at the US Centers for Disease Control and Prevention (CDC) who led the agency's 2004 study on the Measles-Mumps-Rubella (MMR) vaccine and its link to autism.

The scientist, Dr. William Thompson, confessed that the CDC had omitted crucial data in their final report that revealed a causal relationship between the MMR vaccine and autism. Thompson became a whistleblower, announcing there was misappropriation of data on the peer-reviewed studies of autism. He was the author of two of three peer-reviewed epidemiological studies on the American population to prove the safety of Thimerosal. He also co-authored the CDC seminal known as the DeStefano study, which dismissed the link between the MMR vaccine and autism. That study became the foundation for over ninety other studies becoming the cornerstone for claims by the CDC and the vaccine industry that vaccines do not cause Autism.

In 2004, Thompson was ordered by his bosses to withhold data that showed a 340% increased risk of autism on the CDC schedule compared to boys who delayed the MMR vaccine.

Thompson's whistleblower statements were powerful, indeed, as they did find a strong autism signal in children who received the MMR vaccine. But the CDC has systematically concealed the statistical link between vaccines and brain injury.

CDC executives ordered the removal of that data from the final published reports. Dr. Thompson also stated that whenever the CDC finds an adverse effect, the scientists are told to review the data and work out a way where the data can be concealed. For years, these studies were used to prove to the media, doctors, and the general public that the autism link was disproven.

In the Whistle Blower Protection Act and other federal regulations, Dr. Thompson cannot testify under oath without the permission of the director of the CDC, Dr. Thomas Frieden.

At that time, CDC Director Thomas Friedman responded that Dr. Thompson's testimony "Would not substantially promote the objectives of the CDC or HHS" and has refused to allow Dr. Thompson to testify before Congress.

The medical malpractice case seeking Dr. Thompson's testimony is on behalf of sixteen-year-old Yates Hazlehurst. The lawsuit alleges that Yates is autistic as a result of vaccine injuries, which occurred when the vaccines were improperly administered in 2001.

Because of the Vaccine Injury Compensation Act of 1986 (VICA), Hazlehurst v. the Jackson Clinic is the only vaccine injury case that has gone to any U.S. court in thirty years.

It was argued before Tennessee Senior Circuit Court Judge William Acree that Dr. Thompson's testimony was necessary. "Yates, and almost five thousand other vaccine-injured autistic children, lost their cases in vaccine court because the CDC and the Justice Department submitted fraudulent science wrongly denying the vaccine-autism link." Generally, petitions are not adjudicated in the same fiscal year they are filed.

However, the US Department of Health and Human Services subsequently admitted that during the Omnibus Autism Proceeding, it secretly settled and sealed what potentially would have been one of the six test cases, Poling v. HHS after HHS conceded that the vaccines did indeed cause her autism[15]. By conceding the Poling case and opposing the parents' motion for complete transparency, HHS concealed critical evidence of how vaccines can cause autism.

On average, it takes two to three years to adjudicate a petition to the Vaccine Court after it is filed and put forth to a Vaccine Round Table. There is no judge or jury, and the most basic rules of law do not apply.

Over four billion has been paid out to victims of adverse events from vaccines. Over twelve thousand cases have also been dismissed by the court with no compensation.

[15]http://www.huffingtonpost.com/david-kirby/government-concedes-vacci_b_88323.html

- Autism is the fastest-growing developmental disability. (CDC, 2020)
- More than 3.5 million Americans live with an autism spectrum disorder.
- Late 70's there was 1 in ten thousand with Autism
- In the United States, the disability is estimated now at one in fifty-four children. (CDC, 2016)
- In nine years from now, the trend projects a rate of one in three children to be affected.

Diagnosis[16] (from CDC)

- Research has shown that a diagnosis of autism at age 2 can be reliable, valid, and stable.
- Even though ASD can be diagnosed as early as age 2 years, most children are not diagnosed with ASD until after age 4 years. The median age of first diagnosis by subtype is as follows.
    - o Autistic disorder : 3 years, 10 months
    - o ASD/ pervasive developmental disorder (PDD) : 4 years, 8 months
    - o Asperger disorder : 5 years, 7 months
- Studies have shown that parents of children with ASD notice a developmental problem before their child's first birthday. Concerns about vision and hearing were more often reported in the first year, and differences in social, communication, and fine motor skills were evident from 6 months of age.

The CDC points to an 835-page study in 2011 and buried midway in the study was a statement "the evidence is inadequate to accept or reject a cause or relationship the DTAP—(diphtheria, tetanus, pertussis) vaccine and autism. We can neither confirm nor deny".

Epidemiologic And Molecular Relationship Between Vaccine Manufacture And Autism Spectrum Disorder Prevalence

This study[17] served to assess the public health consequences of fetal cell line manufactured vaccines that contain residual human fetal DNA fragments.

[16]https://www.cdc.gov/ncbddd/autism/data.html
[17]https://pubmed.ncbi.nlm.nih.gov/26103708

The study was done on the MMR vaccine and autism disorder and autism spectrum disorder for Norway and Sweden in the UK.

Conclusion: vaccines manufactured in human fetal cell lines contain unacceptably high levels of fetal DNA fragment contaminants. The rest is science.

The Dastardly Defense

Any settlement is not an admission by the United States or the Secretary of Health and Human Services that the vaccine caused the petitioner's alleged injuries, and, in settled cases, the Court does not determine that the vaccine caused the injury. A settlement therefore cannot be characterized as a decision by HHS or by the Court that the vaccine caused an injury.

Standard Of Proof

No-fault vaccine-injury compensation programs are based on the premise that the adverse outcome is not attributable to a specific individual or industry but due to an unavoidable risk associated with vaccines. A problem for all compensation schemes is determining whether there is a causal relationship between a vaccine and a specific injury.

National Vaccine Injury Compensation[18] program Monthly Statistics Report

Fiscal Year	Number of Compensated Awards	Petitioners' Award Amount	Attorneys' Fees/Costs Payments	Number of Payments To Attorneys (Dismissed Cases)	Attorneys' Fees/Costs Payments (Dismissed Cases)
FY 2016	689	$230,140,251.20	$16,225,881.12	99	$2,741,830.10
FY 2017	706	$252,245,932.78	$22,045,785.00	132	$4,444,124.32
FY 2018	521	$199,588,007.04	$16,658,440.14	112	$5,106,382.65
FY 2019	653	$196,217,707.64	$18,991,247.55	102	$4,791,157.52
FY 2020	734	$186,885,677.55	$20,217,550.29	112	$5,650,058.54
FY 2021	330	$114,213,255.48	$12,436,283.17	82	$4,542,814.49
Total	**7,905**	**$4,185,400,226.44**	**$238,717,027.43**	**5,648**	**$95,092,630.28**

[18]https://www.hrsa.gov/vaccine-compensation/data/index.html

Whistleblower: MMR Vaccine

- Two virologists who worked at Merck, Stephen Krahling and Joan Wlochowski, filed a suit that was unsealed in 2010 accusing the company of falsifying its mumps vaccine test results.
- Chatom Primary Care v. Merck & Co. utilizes the same evidence. This is a class-action lawsuit filed "against Merck for unlawfully monopolizing the US market for Mumps Vaccine by engaging in a decade-long scheme to falsify and misrepresent he true efficacy of its vaccine.

It was discovered that the MMR vaccine did not come with an insert—the safety tests and list of potential adverse events. It was the only vaccine that had no safety testing listed on its insert. Did they not do any? Or, what happened? So, the CHD[19] (Children's Health Defense) had to sue the Health and Human Services.

It turns out the safety tests were not the "gold standard" the CDC and FDA talk about. This vaccine had a study group of less than one thousand over a period of two months. There were eight separate tests for one hundred individuals each, for a drug that they intended to give to billions of people.

There are already studies all around the world showing that people who did not have measles as children and were vaccinated for measles have a 67% increased risk of developing non-Hodgkin's lymphoma, and they have a 333% increased risk of developing Hodgkin's lymphoma.

Yet, they want to talk about some immune-suppressed child—the one child out there that may get the measles. In the last 20 years in the US, there has been less than a total of 3000 cases. One death in 2003 and the last one in 2015 as a result of an immune-compromised person. When we hear anything about measles today the media hype describes it as an outbreak and surging cases that measles can cause death. So. if you look at why the measles, mumps, and rubella were combined it is because each disease had such a low risk it would not warrant independent vaccines. Merck's profits were dropping so low

[19]https://childrenshealthdefense.org

by 2007 they had to combine the three to add value and continuance. And they succeeded.

From the book "*Vaccine Epidemic*"

> Mandatory vaccination represents a limitation on human rights. Any limitation such as the rights to liberty, is serious regardless of the supposed public good involved. The United Nations charter has what is called the international Shuman *Bill of Rights* to give more specific definition to the rights and freedoms of people.
>
> The right to vaccination choice is at extreme risk in Canada and the U.S. and in many parts of the world. The American Academy of pediatrics is starting to toe the line of the pharmaceutical companies' message in that no exemption rights should exist. The other conspiring partners in this is a government public health media to our influence and sponsored financially by Pharma.
>
> The number of vaccines that are ready to be executed in the next few years is a long list to be added to the schedule. There will be more efforts by industry and government regarding the adverse events and the liability in the efforts to abolish your rights to choose vaccination.
>
> On the surface for the majority that have no idea of what is in the vaccine, of the adverse events that what it actually does to your system to your body.
>
> There is obviously an overall agenda coming together here. People do not need a vaccine for every disease. There are powerful forces at work but although the pandemic has presented an opportunity for them, the people have more knowledge, more questions, have seen the hypocrisy and now overall transparency is starting to shine through.

6

Eyes Wide Open–The Plan is right in front of us

"It depicted a dark future where technology exists in the public realm only as a tool for the elite to control society."

—George Orwell

- The Number One Conspiracy Target
- The Plan Is Already Here
- The Truth About Philanthropy

Chapter 6

Many books have been written on Bill Gates's significant accomplishments and various (nefarious) agendas. His ingenuity, creativity, and determination brought everyone into the world of computing.

In 2019, at one time, it was the only public company with a market cap of 1 trillion dollars. In 2006, he announced he was leaving his (full time) position at Microsoft to focus on philanthropy. What new culture did he bring over to the Bill and Melinda Gates Foundation and how did he and the foundation become the number one target for conspiracy theories?

First, we need to look at his blueprint for global dominance with Microsoft—what did not go well—and then what lessons, culture, business practices, agenda did he export to the Bill and Melinda Gates Foundation.

Microsoft was fined numerous times for trying to exert its monopoly power. Antitrust, anti-competitive fines were rampant and illegal. In 2000, the company was almost broken up. In the European Union, he was fined $800 million and another $900 million for not complying. In 2013, a fine by the European Commission for $730 million was issued. Tax aversion schemes were rampant.

Attorney Generals of twenty states sued Microsoft for illegally thwarting competition in order to protect and extend its software monopoly.

Business Week Review noted that during court testimony, Bill Gates was called “evasive and nonresponsive” in his testimony. He argued over the definitions of words such as “compete,” “concerned,” “ask,” “we,” and “I don’t recall.”

Pleas of ignorance turned against him when prosecutors showed both sent and received emails regarding many of these concerns: as having stated an intention to “extinguish” and “smother” rival Netscape Communications Corporation. Microsoft was ordered to be split up because it had too much power and control.

Bill Gates stated he, “may have been naïve on how this went down.”

Round one was an attempt at world dominance in technology, but it took a major setback. Round two was a way to us use the billions to slowly infiltrate all areas of global health.

Big Tech had his back, being the strongest players on the planet with the requisite control to censor any negative issues or conspiracies against him. Why? They were in the same game. They provide protection—called censorship. And—Eyes Wide Open—you’ll see we have never seen anything like this censorship in our lifetime.

Just a sample for starters, looking at his Microsoft blueprint. Immense lobbying, grants given to start-ups, funding universities, buying out competitors and complementary companies or companies that would provide backdoor support, leveraging media hype, continuous new versions, leverage technology writers journals, dominant market share, investing in open source platforms whereby thousands of applications could be built on to the operating system, ensuring longevity... the list goes on.

Now think of that if the product was vaccines with control of international health policies, the WHO, media, and a target market of 8 billion people. Add what appears he is laying the groundwork for: control of the food supply (via GMOs) and population control (using 5G networks and other technologies and the ability to monitor vaccine certificates).

"Bill will do whatever is necessary to achieve world domination," says Adobe Systems Vice President Deb Triant, tongue barely in cheek. "For Microsoft, market share was everything."

So, from being sued by the government for breaking the law to parading around as a renowned philanthropist and beacon of altruism, he became intent on ridding the world of disease, setting his sights on a bigger prize.

Use the Blueprint for another Initiative

He has now applied his practices to a world he believes he can control. The plan is actually brilliant. To the untrained eye, it would appear that he is on a mission to help the world, and it is true, but it is being done in his own vision.

Censorship and media only show the positives—that he has placed billions in the hands of the WHO and so many well-deserving organizations—but there are ulterior motives and an endgame.

There has been collateral damage and cost along the way. But you won't know what it is.

Start with population control with his suggestion of a 15% reduction. Many agendas for population control have been in play in some form for a century. *The Open Conspiracy: Blue Prints for a World Revolution*, is a book written H. G. Wells in 1928 about "the scheme to thrust forward and establish human control over the destinies of life."

The OPEN CONSPIRACY is not to be thought of as a single organization. It is a conception of life out of which giant organizations and new orientations will arise conveying the general idea of a world reconstructed. It said, "Help to make over the New World amidst the confusions of the Old."

The parallel is very similar to what we are experiencing today. The World Economic Forum, along with governments and Bill Gates, are calling it The Great Reset. Or it's like an open conspiracy for Bill to move forward with plans presently being activated by the pandemic.

The Rockefeller Foundation has supported depopulation for decades. Their 1968 annual report described their success with reproductive biology that had implications for human fertility and its control.

The Rockefeller's Population Council and the WHO in 1972 created a Task Force on Vaccines for Fertility Regulation. By 1988, a contraceptive implanted under the skin of a woman's upper arm and effective for five years was approved for marketing in twelve countries.

Their further research by 1995, they developed hCG, a hormone secreted into the surface of the early embryo to remain implanted in the womb—preventing them from carrying babies to term. How often was that experiment or clinical trial used on people of third-world countries?

Although forced sterilization without informed consent stopped in the early 1960s, some believe this hormone was a form of eugenics, which was the practice aimed at improving the human population through controlled breeding. All under the guise, of course, of planned parenthood.

What came in the next few decades was a series of scandals over WHO-led vaccination programs in many third-world led to allegations that tetanus vaccines in places were being laced with hCG in order to implement population control by stealth. So much controversy generated by these stories led global institutions to step back from the campaign.

Just a few years ago, a statement by Bill Gates that "if we do a really great job on new vaccines, health care, reproductive health services, we could lower the population by perhaps ten or fifteen percent." That statement has reverberated around the world and poured fuel on what many see as the foundation's overall pattern and agenda. Bill never mentions clean drinking water and proper sanitation that has proven to drastically reduce and eradicate many diseases. The return on investment just isn't there.

Philanthropy

Why is it anyone's business how you use your money? It's your choice what to do with it.

When you practice philanthropy, you get credit and control—you get to decide where the money is going or what project it is for. There is automatic praise on anyone giving money.

Social investment is a strategy and objective aimed at financial return with resultant social good—to select opportunities to profit from that have a significant social impact. Social investment provides those with philanthropic interest the very thing a capitalist needs most: a return on investment (ROI).

The opportunity for philanthropic ROI lies in its donor-investors. That's the pivot wherein a donor actually becomes an investor without abandoning the self-interest that defines investment as an exchange.

Philanthropic ROI applies the principles of social investment to philanthropy with three principles: an economic benefit to the investor, a benefit to an identified group of constituents, and a positive social outcome for society as a whole. The last one is scary in the context of what may come.

When Bill was asked about what he expects as an ROI with his investments in health, vaccines, etc., he openly stated the estimated profitability to be twenty times the investment.

Effectively, BG has moved his track record that set precedents in terms of illegal events in Microsoft to the world of vaccines to a renowned philanthropist and beacon of altruism; but is he truly intent on ridding the world of disease?

Eyes Wide Open - The Microsoft Blueprint

How does Bill get away with so much? Forensic accounting isn't necessary because it is Eyes Wide Open in front of us—for those, at least, that look. Big tech backs him up in the form of censorship. Then, the BG "fact-checkers" are like cleaners. They cherry-pick any negative topics and take them out of context and claim they're false.

Fact checker funding has to come from somewhere. Many are funded by big tech but at arm's length, thus appearing 'independent,' having crafted rules and policies to appear to have no bias. After all, Big Tech needs to protect their own interests, as they are in the business adding vaccine companies to their own portfolios.

The foundation donates billions everywhere, and their public records show where the funds are distributed. There is no covert operation or stealth mode going on. The foundation initiatives are right in front of us. His agenda has been gradually coming to fruition for two decades. On the surface, it appears to be philanthropy in its purest genuine form.

When trying to figure out the foundation, it's like doing a 500-piece table puzzle only to discover that it's only one piece of a much larger puzzle. That's the vastness of where his money flows and to whom it influences.

There is a well-established viewpoint that Gates is using his philanthropy to control WHO, UNICEF, GAVI (Global Alliance for Vaccines and Immunization), and science journalism. His funds go into private pharmaceutical companies that manufacture vaccines and a massive network of pharmaceutical industry front groups that broadcast deceptive propaganda, develop fraudulent studies, and conduct surveillance and psychological operations against vaccine hesitancy. In fact, these are just starting points.

He is second in the world to fund the WHO with billions, and no one gives a check like that without a return.

A recent media blurb: Microsoft - Let's create and infect our computers with a virus and sell an anti-virus. And now–Let's infect people with a virus and then sell a vaccine.

Bill took center stage during the pandemic, assuming a platform that depicted him as a medical expert, though he has no medical expertise. And most of the general public listened. Mainstream media gets the majority of their ad revenue from pharmaceuticals, so it's only reasonable the network handles anything negative gently with soft questions.

Bill gets questions about conspiracies swirling around him like his plans to inject a vaccine with a microchip in it. He denies it, but having the opportunity to really clear these ideas up he seems to just gleam over the subject with complete vagueness. "In a way, it's so bizarre you almost want to see it as something humorous, but it's really not a humorous thing," Gates said.

Where are the tough questions on his foray of experimental vaccines into third-world countries? Some have proven disastrous.

Event 201 - Pandemic Simulation (October 2019)

Bill Gates gave the famous 2015 Ted talk on a pandemic which appears to be a prediction come true, as it is extraordinarily close to the real pandemic.

Then, there was Event 201 gaining so much attention. Coincidently, this timeframe was a month after some authorities were stating the COVID-19 virus actually began.

Event 201 was a simulation of a global corona pandemic—how we would respond—conducted by the Bill & Melinda Gates Foundation, the World Economic Forum, and Johns Hopkins University in October 2019 and included the private sector. There is no evidence that it was meant to model or engineer the current COVID-19 pandemic. In their scenario, a virus killed 65 million people over eighteen months. Before this simulation, it was already known that the world was underprepared for a biological disaster, including the Global Preparedness Monitoring Board.

"The next severe pandemic will not only cause great illness and loss of life but could also trigger major cascading economic and societal consequences that could contribute greatly to global impact and suffering." The Center for Health Security has claimed, "inputs to the model were purely fictional."

Intentional or not, Event 201 "highlighted" the "fictional" challenges of a pandemic, along with recommendations that go hand-in-hand with the great reset agenda that has set up the nefarious "new normal" for all of us.

Microchips

Bill Gates states he doesn't understand this microchip conspiracy. Really?

Maybe it was caused by The CEO of Api-ject. He created a major surge to the microchip conspiracy when explaining their invention, a needle injection system with a vaccine that includes an RFID chip. Obviously, many believed the vaccine was going to have a chip. It was the syringe dispenser that has the RFID chip and not the vaccine. But anyone listening would think that vaccine is going to have a chip. So, that should clear up that theory, right?

Not quite. Why? Because microchips are a reality, and he has investments everywhere to make them a reality.

The USA reported in early June 2020: Gates denies microchip conspiracy theory; Gates statement. "I've never been involved in any sort of microchip-type thing," Gates said in a call with reporters on June 3, adding, "It's almost hard to deny this stuff because it's so stupid or strange." Well, maybe Bill is being naïve again because you actually are involved.

Fridrik Laurusson, an author of the microchip study, is from The Global Good, Intellectual Ventures Laboratory featuring Bill Gates and his extensive involvement.

Approximately $18 million investment in MicroCHIPS Biotech, a company that makes chip-based devices, including birth-control implant chips with wireless on/off switches for remote-controlled drug-delivery.

This is a great example of Bill getting himself into trouble. Did he forget where all his investments and grants are going? Here is a list of a few more where he is involved.

In 2019, according to a *Scientific American* article, Gates commissioned MIT University to build an injectable Quantum dots/nanotechnology dye system to store medical info beneath children's skin and be readable by an iPhone app.

- BG stated, "Keeping track of a child's shots could be so much easier with technology capable of being read by a smartphone."
- Gates's company Microsoft has patented (patent # 060606: "mark of the beast..." that has, on its own, created much controversy) a technology that utilizes implanted chips with sensors that will monitor body and brain activity.
- Investments in Pirbright Institute which researches biological viruses. The institute does hold a patent for a coronavirus that primarily affects chickens.

For any patent to be granted, it must be the first of its kind in the world—for something that does work and has a useful function. Effectively, the patent is an intellectual property claim over our bodies and minds. Bill Gates believes everything can be solved with technology.

Once the Covid vaccine is rolled out, the agenda is to monitor through various certificates. What better way to track, trace, identify, restrict, and segregate people than having the latest technology? For starters;

- In July 2019, before the COVID-19 pandemic, Gates bought 3.5 million shares of Serco, a military contractor with US and UK government contracts, to track and trace pandemic infections and vaccine compliance.
- He invested $1 billion, in EarthNow, which promises to blanket the globe in 5G video surveillance satellites.
- He invested $1 billion in Crown Castle, which owns 5G spy antennas, including more than 40,000 cell towers and 65,000 small cells.
- Bill Gates's 2020 TED talk was edited—to edit out his revealing prediction that we will all soon need digital vaccine passports.
- Gates has said that some kind of "immunity certificate" may be necessary to reopen the economy. "Eventually, what we'll have to have is certificates of who's a recovered person and who's a vaccinated person because you don't want people moving around the world where you'll have some countries that won't have it under control."

As a recap, he (The Foundation) is well-entrenched in influencing global health policies at every level. Significant investments in vaccines, vaccine research and even being on the ground in many countries using his 'platform'. Surveillance technology is in play while Big Tech plays its role in censorship and mainstream media provides the narrative. The microchip is real, and it will first be targeted to third-world countries. In the meantime, our smartphones will serve the gap in between.

Anything read by a smartphone can be monitored by 5G. Next time you use your "smart" device, remember the device is not the product—you are.

In fact, your smartphone already downloaded an application for track and trace purposes. You'll find it in your settings, and it is on behalf of Google. Perhaps that control won't be yours as viruses and vaccines heat up even more. Of course, all tracking would be confidential.

The WEC (World Economic Forum), pharmaceutical companies, and the Bill and Melinda Gates Foundation all have identified that healthy people are the "new" target market for drug and vaccine manufacturers. Our children have now been trained (i.e., indoctrinated) that vaccines are necessary, or our rights and freedoms will be taken. The tremendous success of the COVID-19 narrative has appealed to the hearts of so many. You have only heard it ten thousand times. "You are taking the vaccine to protect others, your community, to reduce hospitalizations, and you are saving lives." You will hear it again because the boosters are coming, and they too will be experimental and need Emergency Use Authorization.

Here is Bill's track record with vaccines:

The Foundation funds the organization GAVI (Global Alliance for Vaccines and Immunization), a global aid organization that specializes in vaccination. BMGF and GAVI are pushing the vaccine agenda with governments around the world with close ties to Pharma companies on its board. Very complex conflict of interest issues have naturally arisen.

Vaccines, for Bill Gates, are a strategic philanthropy that feed his many vaccine-related businesses and give him dictatorial control over global health policy.

Some of the BMGF initiatives with vaccines around the world have landed him and the foundation in controversies and conspiracies.

- Gates became involved with India's National Advisory Board (NAB) with polio vaccines to every child before age five with children then having adverse reactions including death.

- In Nov 2019, WHO stated "More current polio cases have been caused by vaccines than the wild virus: A total of sixteen countries have had outbreaks. The Foundation was central.
- The Foundation funded tests of experimental HPV Human Papilloma Virus vaccines. The vaccine but was canceled in 2010 after hundreds suffered severe side effects, including autoimmune and fertility disorders. Deaths also occurred.
- In 2010, the foundation funded a trial of a GSK's experimental malaria vaccine and has since been blamed for causing serious adverse effects in hundreds of children.
- The foundation is one of the financial supporters for Africa Fact Checkers, providing 11% of its revenue in 2019. The potential to influence or dictate points of view at some level looms large.
- During Gates' 2002 MenAfriVac Campaign in Sub-Saharan Africa, Gates operatives forcibly vaccinated thousands of African children against meningitis. Between 50-500 children developed paralysis. South African newspapers complained, "We are guinea pigs for drug makers."
- Nelson Mandela's former senior economist, Professor Patrick Bond, describes Gates' so-called philanthropic practices as "ruthless" and "immoral."
- In 2014, Kenya's Catholic Doctors Association accused the WHO of chemically sterilizing millions of unwilling Kenyan women with a phony "tetanus" vaccine campaign. Independent labs found the sterility formula in every vaccine tested. After denying the charges, WHO finally admitted it had been developing the sterility vaccines for over a decade. Similar accusations came from Tanzania, Nicaragua, Mexico, and the Philippines.
- A 2017 study showed that WHO's popular DTP (diphtheria, tetanus, pertussis) is killing more Africans than the disease it pretends to prevent. Vaccinated girls suffered 10x the death rate of unvaccinated children.

Regarding the record release of the COVID-19 vaccines, Bill states that, "Traditional vaccine development can take years. Addressing this challenge will take innovation. We need to reimagine the way we use our immune systems to combat disease by creating more vaccines." He may mean the innovation is not to do long-term studies and accept the trade-off for safety for the greater public good.

"The inevitable mass vaccination campaign to eradicate COVID-19 would be the perfect opportunity to introduce a worldwide digital ID. This system would store a wealth of information about each individual (including vaccination history) and would be used to grant access to rights and services."

Bill states that, "if everything went well, it would take eighteen months to get a vaccine." Therapeutics like hydroxyl, remdesivir, and other anti-virals treat someone if they have symptoms only, but they will be in short supply, and the vaccine will be used to prevent the infection. Well Bill, these vaccines do not prevent the infection.

Responding to a question regarding potential compromises in the safety studies, Bill stated, "If you want to wait and see if a side effect occurs later, that takes two or more years".

In my book, *Bitcoin–The Unstoppable Force*, I described where we are heading with the new internet of money known as cryptocurrencies. Over a billion people use only their cell phones for every financial transaction. Sweden, the leading cashless society, has over 10k people with embedded chips in their hand that facilitates transactions for them on buses, trains, and more.

IBM and others have successfully teamed up to have implants in refugees using next-generation encrypted databases referred to as Blockchains. Similar to a debit or credit card, a code-reader allows a screening of the amount of funds the person has to buy food and other items. It also allows government funds to be uploaded from wherever.

The goal of ID2020 is to provide a digital identity from birth, using immunization as the platform for portable, biometrically linked identification.

At Onfido, a tech startup specializing in AI-based biometric ID verification, Gates mentioned, dubbed an "immunity passport." The proposed system would require would-be workers to use the app to scan their face or other biometric data, link that information to a SARS-CoV-2 antibody test (or, eventually proof of coronavirus vaccination), and then have their picture taken and immunity verified every time they wish to access a restricted space or work environment.

A decade ago, the government of India began what has been called "The Largest Social Experiment on Earth," enrolling over one billion people in the largest biometric identification database ever constructed. All biometric details are recorded in a centralized database, and citizens are issued a twelve-digit identity number that would prove identity and vaccination among other personal details.

Aadhaar app is entirely based on using biometrics to ensure uniqueness. The ten fingerprints of both the hands, the iris of both the eyes, and a photograph.

Unsurprisingly, the company receives support from the Bill and Melinda Gates Foundation through its involvement in the GSMA Inclusive Tech Lab. And now, Gates is funding a retool of Aadhaar for a global rollout.

The Indian experiment in pioneering this biometric digital economy—an experiment with which Gates has been so intimately involved—also provides a perfect example of just how such a system will be abused. There have been structural flaws, security vulnerabilities and the emerging mass identification databases are creating privacy issues. IDs that have been breached are sold openly.

It does have nightmarish implications for this type of all-seeing, all-pervasive society where every transaction and every movement of every citizen is monitored, analyzed, and databased in real-time by the government.

So, how does all of this tie in with the foundation's interests and investments with chemical giant Monsanto, which lost a $10 billion court case on health hazards of glyphosate/round-up. In his book, Gates describes his plan for climate change and changing the life of farmers in Africa with the use of GMOs. But many of the companies he invests in like Yara makers of synthetic fertilizer produce more greenhouse gas than his climate change plans to "decrease."

His open plan for Western nations to switch to a diet of 100% synthetic beef is equally insane. This may be why he now buying up cattle farms in the US, becoming the largest private owner with a strategy to control the meat supply, making meat a luxury. GMO food-based products and synthetic meat sound more like a recipe that is just downright unhealthy. But all of that can be supported with new drugs and vaccines to a much bigger global target market.

As we can see, many pieces of the puzzle are coming together—and the image is draconian.

7

The Roadmap & The Prediction

"All truths are easy to understand once they are discovered; the point is to discover them."

—Galileo Galilei

- Tony Fauci Prediction
- Dangerous Research - Self Spreading Vaccines
- CDC Failings

Chapter 7

Is there is a conspiracy with this pandemic or has this at least laid the groundwork for an ulterior plan using it as positioning for something already in play? What would be opportunistic here? Who would be the major players with the most to gain be?

In any crime, collusion, conspiracy, or conflict of interest there is always a motive. Just follow the money. What can be gained and more importantly what is the end game.

How is possible to actually plan a pandemic? Some have called it a plandemic.

Governments sit at the top of the food chain. They need to appeal to the people but also need to stay in power. (It is obvious that Pharma leads the pack with the most to gain)

In virology, gain-of-function research is employed to better understand current and future pandemics. In vaccine development, gain-of-function research is conducted to gain a head start on a virus and to develop a vaccine or relevant therapy in the meantime.

Then-CDC Director Dr. Julie Gerberding reiterated the importance of open access to the virus and its genome at a press conference.

> "The concern that the federal government is looking at right now is that we could be locked out of this opportunity to work with this virus if it's patented by someone else," Gerberding wrote. "By initiating steps to secure patent rights, we assure that we will be able to continue to make the virus and the products from the virus available in the public domain and that we can continue to promote the rapid technological transfer of this biomedical information into tools and products that are useful to patients.

"From our standpoint, it's a protective measure to make sure that the access to the virus remains open for everyone," she added, noting that the CDC had published the genome on its website.

That practice is known as "defensive patenting." So wait, the CDC has patents on vaccines? Let's backtrack to the start of the origination.

Gain Of Function

The public health danger from the escape, from laboratories, of viruses capable of causing pandemics has become the subject of considerable, well-merited discussion, spurred by "gain of function" experiments. The goal of these experiments—in which researchers manipulate already dangerous pathogens to create or increase communicability among humans—is to develop tools to monitor the natural emergence of pandemic strains. And in the last decade, there are many scientists not being recognized that have stated this is dangerous research.

The significant risk is not hypothetical.

These arguments appear in a variety of recent research papers, including Rethinking Biosafety in Research on Potential Pandemic Pathogens; The Human Fatality and Economic Burden of a Man-made Influenza Pandemic:

> *A Risk Assessment; Containing the Accidental Laboratory Escape of Potential Pandemic Influenza Viruses; and Response to Letter by the European Society for Virology on "Gain-of-Function" Influenza Research.*

In 2014, the National Institutes of Health proclaimed to believe there were legal and moral issues with its research on coronaviruses in the U.S., which motivated scientists and the NIH to transfer this research to China.

The funding was halted in 2014 because of the efforts to make three viruses more deadly. The common flu, Mers, and Sars. Seriously? They tried to make them worse?

As this book is in writing the true story has become a moving target but more will have been exposed on the gain of research funding. Tony Fauci oversees six billion dollar budget for the National Institute of Allergy and Infectious Disease.

The funding for gain of research through EcoHealth Alliance which Tony Fauci denied in Congress from Senator for the Wuhan Lab was Doctor Rand Paul.

EcoHealth Alliance under questioning has received NIH funding for this work since 2008, amounting to $5.96 million over twelve years, according to NIH data.

On Dec 19, 2017, for some reason, the US government lifted its controversial ban on funding experiments that make certain pathogens more deadly or transmissible. The National Institutes of Health announced that scientists can once again use federal money to conduct gain-of-function research on pathogens such as influenza viruses with a new framework for safety.

The US government lifted a three-year ban on making lethal viruses in the lab, saying the potential benefits of disease preparedness outweigh the risks. Dr. Francis S Collins, Head of The NIH, stated that "such work will now proceed but only if a scientific panel to assess benefits versus the risks in this controversial research." Scientists have thus been permitted to make lethal strains of illnesses despite the fear of accidental outbreaks.

It applies to viruses and other pathogens that have the potential to kill thousands, if not millions, of people worldwide.

Other projects remained blocked, including controversial efforts to alter bird flu viruses to understand the genetic changes that may make it easier for them to infect people. Supporters of this research argue that it's necessary to understand the threat posed by natural viral mutation.

The world of science is split on this. "I worry about the future of this work," says Gigi Kwik Gronvall of the Johns Hopkins Center for Health Security. And there is a lot to worry about.

There is a long lineup of science critics that question whether the benefits outweigh the possibility of an accidental release of a virus that could kill on a huge scale. "There is a small subset of science where, if you mess up, you jeopardize large, large numbers of people," says Marc Lipsitch, an epidemiologist at the Harvard T.H. Chan School of Public Health.

Then, there is the question of how to control access to the data that could provide the recipe for a deadly bioweapon. Unlike nuclear physicists, who for decades have accepted that some of their work must be classified, biologists are used to publishing their results in scientific journals without restraint.

There has been a long, fierce debate about making more pathogens more deadly. Critics say such gain-of-function research still risks creating an accidental pandemic.

Marc Lipsitch, an epidemiologist at the Harvard T.H. Chan School of Public Health in Boston, Massachusetts, says that gain-of-function studies "have done almost nothing to improve our preparedness for pandemics—yet they risked creating an accidental pandemic."

Fifty-four scientists have lost their jobs as a result of an NIH probe into foreign ties.

By Jeffrey Mervis (Jun. 12, 2020)

Since 2007, the US government has required companies, universities, federal agencies, and non-profits that sponsor clinical trials to report their results, whether positive, negative, or inconclusive, so that doctors, patients, and researchers can learn about the safety and efficacy of new drugs or devices. While it has taken some ten years to start enforcing, the NIH Director Francis Collins warned trial sponsors that if they violate the reporting law, they would be listed on a ClinicalTrials.gov "wall of shame." There has been improved reporting but for thousands of trials, sponsors still ignore the law.

Congress created the reporting law after pharma companies continued to suppress data revealing lucrative drugs to be unsafe or ineffective.

In 2017, the FDA and the National Institutes of Health released a "final rule" to clarify the requirements and the penalties for ignoring them.

Would it not bring into question Trump's announcement of Warp Speed by year-end? He became under attack on all fronts from science, mainstream media, democrats, and perhaps lack of confidence from the public. No vaccine has ever been developed in this timeline. Perhaps, this was the attack opportunity the democrats needed as elections drew closer.

What can anyone draw from Tony Fauci association with Moderna? That is too extensive to write about, Moderna has done extensive research on mRNA but have never manufactured a vaccine for public use. So, we have a 60-year history of pharmaceutical companies making vaccines, and now Moderna gets the green light to vax the global population with the first-ever vaccine with of course Emergency Use. Did Moderna say to Tony Fauci–hey we're all set with our mRNA vaccine–so let's run with it?

Hard to believe. So how was it that clinical trials were being ramped up by Moderna in April/May, just six weeks after border closure? Was this a connection to all of this being part of a plandemic? Mostly because it wasn't planned but became a once-in-a-lifetime opportunity for who: there is a long list to whom the beneficiaries will be.

Tony Fauci/Sandeep Singh/Bill Gates all stated it would be at least 18 months and more before a vaccine could be done under all initiatives. They have made their concerns clear about the safety, and of course, Bill Gates has clearly stated that there will be some safety trade offs. Later, Bill Gates stated, we know the clinical trials were a large, randomized clinical group—one with limited scope due to warp speed (i.e., no accounting for pregnant women/co-morbidities/ thrombosis, people with diabetes) and lacked the standard animal testing. Obviously, no long--term study could be performed either, and there may never be one. The control group that received the placebo is being pushed to take the vax. So, how can you conclude a clinical trial for long-term implications? You can't and this once again proves that gold standard of vaccine study and safety from the CDC/FDA rarely happens. If long-term study is not in play there will be no evidence of potential future adverse events. In three, five, or eight years, there will be no determination regarding long-term safety results. This means we will have nothing to compare to the 170 adverse events already listed and now you can add blood clots to the list. These adverse events will be looked upon as correlation is not causation. The same will happen with the lineup of bi-annual boosters being prepared for all.

In an unprecedented enforcement action, the FDA informed a clinical trial sponsor that it had violated the law by requiring that results from human studies of medical treatments and devices be posted to the federal repository clinical trials[20]. The action was leveled against the Cambridge, Massachusetts–based drug company Acceleron Pharma for its failure to provide data from a completed trial of its experimental drug to treat kidney cancer.

In other investigations by the NIH, some 285 grants by the NIH totaling $164 million

So, what was the nature of the violations that NIH has uncovered? The researchers /Big Pharma/universities: failed to disclose to NIH the receipt of a foreign grant; failed to disclose participation in a foreign talent program like China's 'thousands talent plan'; hid ties to a foreign company; and buried foreign patent and violations of NIH's science peer-review system.

The NIH has now been in the forefront of federal efforts to identify and block behavior that many US government officials say poses a significant threat to the country's economic well-being and to national security. Several bills pending in Congress seek to limit that threat in various ways, including by limiting the flow of scientific talent from China to the United States, and by restricting access to federally funded research that provides a foundation for cutting-edge technologies and new industries. This may include Tony Fauci's funding overseas.

In the NIH broader investigation, they have flagged 399 scientists "*of possible concern*" to NIH, and the FBI has fingered 121 of

[20]https://clinicaltrials.gov/ct2/home

them. Another fifty have been flagged by their own institutions. The NIH is making inquiries to major U.S. research universities asking them to provide information about specific faculty members with NIH funding who are believed to have links to foreign governments.

NIH's response to demands from members of Congress and national security officials that federal agencies do a better job of monitoring any foreign interactions fostered by US government funding.

In August 2020, NIH Director Francis Collins was to give clear directives on standards to more than 10,000 institutions, stating "threats to the integrity of US biomedical research exist" and highlighted the failure to disclose "substantial resources from other organizations, including foreign governments." The goal is to prevent the theft of intellectual property and the transfer of technologies that could threaten U.S. security.

Scientists are working on a vaccine that spreads like a disease, but it's called a self-spreading vaccine. It's more than just a concept.

The logistical challenge to vaccinating billions of people along with all the ethical questions is something we all have seen or experienced. Emerging diseases are around the corner, and as Bill Gates stated, "The next one will be ten times worse." But what if these complicated and resource-intensive issues were implemented? John Hopkins University put forth reports on such technologies to address the global catastrophic biological risks.

With self-spreading vaccines that are genetically engineered to move through populations like communicable diseases but instead provide protection, only a small number of individuals in a target population would need to be vaccinated.

The virus strain would then circulate like a pathogenic virus, resulting in widespread immunity. This would be used in the event of a major public health event, thus eliminating the need for mass vaccination operations.

The flu vaccine can be used as a reasonable comparison. After receipt of the flu vaccine, shedding of the live attenuated vaccine virus to unvaccinated persons is common. Hospitals and clinics will sometimes post a notice to stay out of specific areas if you have had the flu shot in the last fourteen days.

Shedding stops in most cases by eleven days post-vaccination with much lower shedding percentages by fourteen days. Since the rollout of COVID-19, there are myriad reports of shedding. However, the science will tell us there is no scientific evidence, as it is all antidotal.

Well, pretty much everything about the new vaccines is antidotal because it is a moving target and this was not in the scope of the clinical trials—nor is it being monitored currently.

What could go possibly go wrong? There have been other vaccines that have caused the vaccine virus to revert to the wild-type virulence, meaning actually creating more disease than the vaccine is supposed to prevent.

Well, just based on the first thought of this being used as a biological weapon is one factor. However, from "the science perspective," this would be a medical risk and a public perception risk to the public. The possibility of a vaccine-induced disease would have major public acceptance.

How would Big Pharma get their return on investment? Since there would be no injections, there is no cost per needle. Just like the governments today providing hundreds of billions to fund the development of Sars Cov-2 through taxpayers' dollars, the profit picture would be based on the numbers in a specific target population.

Fauci

Anthony S. Fauci, MD, director of the National Institute of Allergy and Infectious Diseases, (NIAID) was a Keynote speaker at Georgetown University on Jan 10, 2017.

> *"There is no doubt Donald J. Trump will be confronted with a surprise infectious disease outbreak during his presidency."*

Fauci warned that preventing disease pandemics often starts overseas. "We will definitely get surprised in the next few years," he said. "Risks have never been higher." The thing we're extraordinarily confident about is that we're going to see this in the next few years." Is he that skilled, knowledgeable, or does he have a greater insight into epidemiology? Perhaps Fauci understands more than most—that there are frequent lab escapes from facilities like the Wuhan lab.

His speech is still available on many websites but it has gone down the "memory hole" meaning it has been scrubbed by Big Tech from the internet.

Dr. Anthony Fauci, director of the National Institute of Allergy and Infectious Diseases (NIAID), said in the lead-up to the SARS outbreak in 2002-2003, his agency devoted between $3 million and $5 million a year to research into the coronavirus family.

After the explosive SARS outbreak, which infected more than 8,000 people and killed nearly 800 worldwide, NIAID coronavirus funding increased tenfold, rising to a high of $51 million a year later but then dropping off.

The emergence of the new virus is going to change that figure, likely considerably, Fauci said. "I don't know how much it's going to be. But I think it's going to generate more sustained interest in coronaviruses because it's very clear that coronaviruses can do really interesting things."

Fauci, The Prescient

Sars Coronavirus Patent[21]–1 Year Before

It is particularly problematic for U.S. Patent 10,702,600 ('600), which is the patent relating to, "a messenger ribonucleic acid (mRNA) comprising an open reading frame encoding a beta coronavirus (BetaCoV) S protein or S protein subunit formulated in a lipid nanoparticle." The specific claims addressing the pivot to the SARS Coronavirus were patented on March 28, 2019—nine months before the SARS CoV-2 breakout.

Their "emergence" by accident or design from a lab where humans are creating them is far more likely than a pathogenic virus emerging through the slow, haphazard process of evolution and then finding a human to attach to.

There is agreement among many scientists that the odds of a natural pandemic vs. a manmade one are very small. Concerned scientists

[21]https://www.scribd.com/document/491324739/The-Fauci-COVID-19-Dossier

have argued in statistical detail that the risk of an epidemic coming out of a lab producing dangerous viruses is high compared to a rare emergence from nature.

If we fast-forward to 2021 and look at the investigation of the Wuhan Lab, we know there was a handpicked team by the WHO and China which included one handpicked sketchy representative from the US. After a thorough 2-hour lab review, not a week but a few hours, including consulting with lab technicians. Their conclusion: "It did not come from the high-security Level 4 biological lab in Wuhan, and escapes are an extreme rarity." Would this not be a time and a reason for government and media to rise up and demand why this has not been fully challenged and investigated? To identify the source of the overall impact of lockdowns we experienced and what is coming. Maybe it is just being left the so-called radicals. The people that question; the people who are stigmatized, the conspiracy theorist groups, or in this case, the people who stand for freedom, transparency and are pro-truth.

The majority of science whistleblowers point to a Wuhan lab escape. The former CDC director Robert Redfield gave his opinion in an interview with Sanjay Gupta who everyone knows is the CNN science/doctor specialist who has no patients - believes the same, which is why the WHO and twenty-nine nations except New Zealand are now taking a collaborative exception to this report.

Shouldn't we all know at this point? Shouldn't every person in the world—every government and every scientist—demand a proper investigation? What exactly is being created in these labs? And for what purpose?

The truth is, escapes are not rare. There is actually a long list of escapes from secure labs.

Many other laboratory escapes of high-consequence pathogens have occurred, resulting in transmission beyond laboratory personnel. Ironically, these laboratories were working with pathogens to prevent the very outbreaks they ultimately caused. For that reason, the tragic consequences have been called "self-fulfilling prophecies." The science is firm on this much. Perhaps this is Fauci's insight.

From 1938 to 1972, the VEE vaccine (Venezuelan Equine Encephalitis) caused most of the very outbreaks that it was called upon to prevent, a clear self-fulfilling prophecy.

A laboratory escape occurred in March 1972. A lab assistant at the London School of Hygiene and Tropical Medicine, while harvesting a live smallpox virus from eggs used as a growing medium became infected and was hospitalized. But before she was placed in isolation, she infected two visitors to a patient, both of whom died.

In August of 1978, a medical photographer at a lab at Birmingham Medical School developed smallpox and died due to an escape.

In 1995, a major VEE animal and human outbreak struck Venezuela and Colombia. There were at least 10,000 human VEE cases with eleven deaths in Venezuela and an estimated 75,000 human cases in Colombia, with 3,000 neurological complications and 300 deaths. VEE virus was isolated from ten stillborn or miscarried human fetuses. The major scientific group working on VEE published a paper in 2001 stating the 1995 outbreak most likely was a laboratory escape.

The swine flu scare of 1976 and the H1N1 human influenza pandemic of 1977 tell a similar tale.

In 1976, the H1N1 swine influenza virus struck New Jersey, causing thirteen hospitalizations and one death. That year, fears of a swine flu pandemic had loomed large with 200 infected. President Gerald Ford had ordered an unprecedented mass vaccination of everyone in the United States. Panic spread amongst the entire American population based on ill-founded science and political interests. This triggered a potential unprecedented pandemic, and there was an effort to vaccinate all Americans. No swine H1N1 pandemic materialized, but there was a high level of complications in terms of adverse effects—including death.

Later, researchers discovered that benign swine flu strains had been circulating in the US population long before this one was identified.

The 1977 pandemic spread rapidly worldwide but was limited to those under twenty years of age. Older persons were immune from exposures before 1957. But it caused a mild disease, and fatalities were few.

The consequences of the escape of a highly lethal avian virus with enhanced transmissibility would almost certainly be much graver than the 1977 escape of a "seasonal," possibly attenuated strain to a population with substantial existing immunity.

SARS outbreaks after the SARS epidemic provide such insight. The 2003 Severe Acute Respiratory Syndrome outbreak spread to twenty-nine countries, causing more than 8,000 infections and at least 774 deaths. SARS has not re-emerged naturally, but there have been six escapes from virology labs: one each in Singapore and Taiwan, and four separate escapes at the same laboratory in Beijing.

Foot and mouth disease in the UK in 2007 provides another illustration. Foot and Mouth Disease (FMD) infects cloven-hoofed animals such as pigs, sheep, and cattle. It has been eradicated in North America and most of Europe. In 2001, however, a UK outbreak resulted in ten million animals being killed.

In 2007, FMD appeared again in Britain, four kilometers from a biosafety level 4 laboratory—a designation indicating the highest level of lab security—located at Pirbright.

The strain had caused a 1967 outbreak in the United Kingdom but was not then circulating in animals anywhere. It was, however, used in vaccine manufacture at the Pirbright facility. What a surprise. Pirbright is funded by Bill Gates.

The general public never really hears about these types of stories from the mainstream. But we do hear on international news that there was a bus accident sliding off a cliff injuring 5 people in a country most would not recognize.

These narratives of escaped pathogens have common themes. There are unrecognized technical flaws in standard biocontainment, as demonstrated in the UK smallpox and FMD cases. Inadequately inactivated preparations of dangerous pathogens are handled in laboratory areas with reduced biosecurity levels, as demonstrated in the SARS and VEE escapes. In 2010, 244 unintended releases of bioweapon candidate "select agents" were reported.

In coronavirus research in the late 1990s, the only known human coronaviruses were ones that cause colds—not the highest scientific imperative.

Intro To COVID-19 Roadmap

Did the lockdowns beginning in March of 2020 mean anything? By that time, over five million people had traveled from Wuhan to all parts of the world. China had closed air transportation to their own provinces within the country, but they left international transportation hubs open. Why would they do that?

While China continued to protest international travel bans, it successfully quarantined Wuhan and other affected cities. The total domestic lockdown of Hubei province and the flight ban imposed inside China had an immediate effect. As per data from the public access on traffic statistics, the TomTom Traffic Index website showed Wuhan had a traffic density of 60% in January while Shanghai and Beijing had nearly 80% density.

After the total lockdown, the average traffic density fell to below 10% in Wuhan and Shanghai during February and below 5% in Beijing. While implementing a total domestic lockdown in February, China kept assuring the world that the situation was not serious and fully under control.

The Wuhan Institute has been known as "a center of China's declared biowarfare/biodefense capacity." Its director comes from China's biological warfare program, as confirmed in a report stating "China 'appoints its top military bio-warfare expert to take over secretive virus lab in Wuhan.' "

No one can hold high positions or conduct research at the Wuhan Institute of Virology without being closely involved with and supervised by the military.

In February 2021, after more than one full year of the pandemic alert, the head of WHO's inspection team Peter Ben Embarek and his staff were allowed into the China Lab. It took one year for this inspection with little to no media coverage of the origins. In fact, when Trump stated he believed it came from the Wuhan lab he was crucified.

If a fire breaks out, you know there will be a fire investigation, which is done the next day or when the area is secure. This is just a fire. Here we have a global crisis and nothing?

Here, we are dealing with the worst pandemic in our time, and we can't even investigate the potential cause. For a year the general public, the mainstream media, and mainstream scientists were not talking about it. At least now in July 2021 mainstream and government are having conversations.

Biosafety incidents involving regulated pathogens are occurring on average over twice a week in the U.S. alone. Such incidents have included the mishandling of agents as deadly as anthrax, smallpox, and bird flu. And, as is well known, a virology lab in Beijing managed to accidentally release the original SARS virus (SARS1) not once but four separate times.

Still more astonishingly, though, according to Gary Shih of the Washington Post, Peter Ben Embarek, in explaining why the WHO team had ruled out the lab leak hypothesis, said that it was largely a result of questioning Wuhan lab staff about what they thought about such a possibility. "They're the best ones to dismiss the claims and provide answers to all the questions," Dr. Embarek said.

The lengths that China is going to in order to control the WHO's narrative was highlighted in John Sudworth's report on the press conference for the BBC. It showed Chinese officials prevented him from interviewing a WHO team member after the press conference. The Washington Post's Josh Rogin tweeted in response to it, "This entire WHO field trip is a farce and a huge missed opportunity to conduct a genuine investigation, which a year into the crisis Beijing will still not allow."

To some degree it appears to be purposely executed by China allowing international travel to continue, knowing that the disease can be carried with those travelers—in a large portion to your country.

But there is evidence it occurred earlier than Dec 2019. Robert Redfield, former CDC Director believes it started as early as September.

How, then, weren't China's advanced systems triggered? China's earlier experiences with SARS outbreaks prompted them to implement a specifically designed reporting system that could notify all health authorities of potential health situations within twenty-four hours. This has been further enhanced with their rollout of the 5G network and 30k cameras in the Wuhan province feeding their Ai network. With a decade of refining this system, how would it be possible new diseases would not be known by to have human to human transmission.

So, what happened in this case? Where was their transparency? And on another note, why does China only give one-tenth of the funding the US does? So here is the general timeline:

Dec. 31- COVID-19 is first detected in Wuhan, China, and is reported by Chinese authorities to the World Health Organization.

Jan 14 - Maria D Van Kerkhove (WHO)states that there is no clear evidence of human-to-human transmission.

Jan 18 - Trump gets an intelligence briefing warning threat the Chinese officials appeared to be minimizing the severity of the outbreak.

Jan 20 - China TV acknowledges human-to-human transmission

Jan 23 - China publicly notifies the WHO that human-to-human transmission is a reality.

But wait. The Chinese New Year was about to happen and start the largest migration on the planet—50-100 million traveling throughout China in celebration and many going around the world.

Strict quarantine measures were in place in February in Wuhan with a complete lockdown implemented on January 23.

Scheduled domestic travel was severely limited, but international travel was still allowed and encouraged. Wait, they allowed potentially infected people to travel while they locked down domestic residents? Aviation data from major airlines indicate that more than 5000 people traveled to the US alone just before the travel ban.

On January 30, the WHO declared a public health emergency of international concern.

Jan. 31 - Trump announced the ban on the admission of people/ flights from China, effective February 2. Trump was deemed a racist by the Democrats and many around the world but later received modest applause he did the right thing

Feb. 29 - The WHO speaks out against the ban from China, stating that, "travel or trade restrictions related to COVID-19 outbreaks are usually not effective in preventing the importation of cases but may have a significant economic and social impact."

HELLO. What about a lockdown that followed?

The WHO director, General Tedros, supported China's assertion, quoted saying, "There is no reason for measures that unnecessarily interfere with international travel and trade. We call on all countries to implement decisions that are evidence-based and consistent." The WHO/Chinese regime kept assuring the world that the outbreak was fully under control.

In China, domestic travel was severely limited, but international travel did not drop off until late March.

Was China Saving Face?

It's only a few million in the Chinese Communist Party (CCP) that truly control the 1.4 billion people via dictatorship. The CCP's political power was the most important thing. economic operations took priority; therefore, they let international flights go. Did they want to spread the virus to the rest of the world?

Economic profit appears to be have been more important than people's lives. Was there intent to spread the virus because they were being hit hard or just negligence in keeping up the economy?

The only country in the world to have its GDP increase in 2020 was China.

The Vaccine Agenda Is Starting To Unfold

The CDC, government officials, the pharmaceutical industry, and the mainstream media are capitalizing on the coronavirus pandemic to further their ongoing agenda and eliminate any remaining opposition that may be in a position to fight back. What opposition? And to what end?

Unfortunately, the organizations that are supposed to protect us may be using us as pawns in the war on freedom by the elite. You see, it is well understood that there has been an agenda for years now to force vaccines and other pharmaceutical interventions on all citizens. Bill Gates says it's best—we need to have a vaccine for everyone on the planet. This may be the foundation for the rollout of over 150 vaccines that are at some level of research and clinical trial.

After all, these drugs generate obscene amounts of profit. Mandating them would create, at best, guaranteed ten-fold profits with the customer base as customers for life.

"The WHO... they called it wrong," said President Trump. "They missed the call. They should have called it months earlier. They would have known. They should have known. And they probably did know. So we will be looking into that very carefully, and we are going to put a hold on money spent to the WHO."

Even mainstream media sources who are normally critical of Trump admit that the WHO's stance being in line with China is investigation-worthy. But mainstream media changes on a dime.

"Institutions of international governance are prone to a particular form of corruption: they're inclined to serve powerful interests at the expense of their mission," wrote journalist Robert Wright in an April 10 article for Wired magazine.

So, what happened before the recognition that we had a major outbreak on our hands?

Did the communist government withhold information about the severity of the coronavirus outbreak so it would have time to hoard medical supplies? The intelligence reports from the US Department of Homeland Security might confirm that.

Before sharing full details on the novel coronavirus outbreak with the WHO, Beijing dramatically increased its imports and decreased its exports of medical supplies.

In January, according to the World Trade Organization that reports on global trade, China increased its imports of surgical face masks by 278%, surgical gowns by 72%, and surgical gloves by 3%.

Meanwhile, it slashed its global exports of a wide range of medical products: surgical gloves by 48%, surgical gowns by 76%, surgical gloves by 32%, medical ventilators by 45%, incubator kits by 56%, thermometers by 53%, and cotton balls and swabs by 58%.

Back To Fauci

What do we know about Fauci? He has become front-line center as the go-to person. He has one opinion: his. How is he one of the few politicians (science politicians) to stay in the same position of power through six government changes over the course of forty years? How was he allowed to be the only spokesperson to have economic control; have education control; have our livelihoods controlled all in the form of lockdown. He has stated children are not affected but locked them out of the classroom and more.

Fauci holds himself out as the ultimate source of objective scientific information and science-based conclusions. He is well connected with Pharma, has received royalties on vaccines, and controlled modest funding to the Wuhan Lab. He also mandated no other treatments to be used in and authorized hospitals, clinics, and more. Many doctors moved ahead anyway with safe, off-label treatments that when applied early, there was a great success.

I asked my doctor if I got Covid what is the treatment? Quarantine and perhaps take Ibuprofen. "Can you prescribe any other treatments like hydroxyC and others? No. Can you refer me to a physician that can? No. And if it gets really worse, then come to the hospital. Vitamin D, Zinc, C not even a mention. I asked about treatment packs that dozens of other countries were using and they were unknown to him. Last question why can't you prescribe these safe medications? Health authorities have mandated it.

So until you can't breathe, then go to emergency where various cocktails are given then to ventilators. Fauci has appeared to have suppressed the most effective, safest, and least expensive medication treatment (hydroxychloroquine in varied combinations) while manipulating his clinical research to promote an ineffective, dangerous, and highly expensive drug (remdesivir). This is well documented.

So Fauci has been considered a top-level expert in his field and has been given the platform to express this.

Some say in reality, he works with and empowers globalist pharmaceutical firms and globalist organizations such as WHO and the Bill and Melinda Gates Foundations.

Meanwhile, these globalists gained power and influence as their policies and practices, including the shutdowns, continue to worsen conditions throughout the world.

In early June 2021, ICAN–The Informed Consent Action Network through The Freedom of Information Act requested Tony Fauci's emails but were denied by the NIH. ICAN had to make a legal challenge and won. There are several thousand emails now on the ICAN website and more coming exposing Fauci's mistruths. One mistruth is about masks and now we know why Fauci, The Surgeon General of the US for example, continued to flip-flop on the validity of masks. On 60 Minutes, he basically stated masks don't work. Sometime later, two masks are better than one. His specific email looked like this: March 21, 2020–In Fauci's email in reference to 9 different studies on masks, "generally there were not a lot of differences in flu rates when masks were used". Congress is now cross examining him for the second time.

In another email an excerpt from April 2020, they treated the first group of five patients a potent antiaggregant therapy (Tirofiban/ Aggrastat), and apparently in all of them the P02 stated to rise within less than 2 hours, they got off the ventilator and went on to a full recovery.

What? Fauci was made known about an early treatment that was given to people that were on ventilators and fully recovered–when at that time there were - 9 out of 10 people who died when on a ventilator. Why didn't we hear about that? Cameron Kyle-Sidell, MD in NY, April 2020 identified ventilators were killing people–that they needed oxygen, not ventilation. He did not do well after going on social media.

What other treatments were being discussed that they knew about but were never put out? There were many Doctors who used hydroxychloroquine with great success as long it was used in the early stages. The Doctors who used Ivermectin and even reported to Congress were showing an 85% reduction in hospitalizations and deaths. What about quertin, zinc, and Vitamin D?

The Food and Drug Administration (FDA) approved emergency use of hydroxychloroquine for a short time. After a study found no evidence that the drug could stop deaths or help people with COVID-19 get better faster. That more research is needed and Tony Fauci, CDC, FDA, WHO shut down the use for this Covid treatment.

If you investigate that lightning-fast study, it would show hydroxyl was administered in extremely high doses and at a time when the patient's conditions were severe. It was not used appropriately and doomed to fail.

So, here's the thing. The vaccines for Covid19 being rolled out could not get EUA Emergency Use Authorization from the FDA unless there was no other treatment available. Get the connection? What if there was a way to block other treatments? Would pharma make more, less, or no money if these treatments work? Science advisors are stating there are not enough studies to use medications yet they have been used for decades. So, if there are potential life-saving treatments with medications with proven use for decades that if used early to treat for C19, wouldn't you want to know about it? And most likely you would want access? How is it that Doctor's take the oath "Do no harm" and then tell their patient there is nothing they can do until you turn blue.

Well, there are thousands of doctors around the globe who defied that order and had great success. Think of how many lives that could have been saved.

Back to other emails from Tony Fauci, that have interesting connections with Bill Gates and the Foundation back in April 2020 looking at the synergies to promote the vaccines globally.

So, what if it turns out that through all the data or some acknowledgment by high-level senior health advisors that C19 is actually a severe seasonal flu and that masks are relatively ineffective?

Neil Ferguson

Neil Ferguson catapulted the world. He created the model that locked down the world, helping to shape the policy right from the start.

By the end of March, governments had moved or were about to move into the first-ever lockdown. Along with that was a campaign of fear.

That prediction by Neil Ferguson—that half a million would die in the UK and more than two million in the US—was used to justify a myriad draconian measures.

Ferguson is the same authority that predicted 136,000 deaths due to mad cow disease, 200,000 deaths due to avian flu, and 65,000 due to swine flu. He was wildly wrong every time.

NF, who was a strong advocate of the lockdown in the UK, resigned—after he was found to be breaking his own lockdown rules. He wasn't the first and we all witnessed many politicians having dinner parties, traveling and breaking many lockdown rules. You can see they were really taking it seriously.

His modeling projected an astounding 4% global death. The famed 2.2 million death rate for the US estimate first reached viral status in the March 31 White House briefing by doctors Anthony Fauci and Deborah Birx.

The severity and breadth of those statewide shutdowns were justified by just one dramatic statistic.

The March 16 paper forecast that in a scenario without interventions, 81% of the UK population would become infected and that 0.9% of them would die (i.e., 610,000 fatalities). That was the scenario that bounced the UK government into changing its approach.

Professor Neil Ferguson has given an extraordinary interview to Tom Whipple at The Times, in which he confirms the degree to which he believes that imitating China's lockdown policies at the start of 2020 changed the parameters of what Western societies consider acceptable.

"I think people's sense of what is possible in terms of control changed quite dramatically between January and March," Professor Ferguson says. SAGE, the organization that studies perspectives of international scope - observed the "innovative intervention" out of China, of locking entire communities down and not permitting them to leave their homes, they initially presumed it would not be an available option in a liberal Western democracy:

> *"It's a communist one-party state, we said. We couldn't get away with it in Europe, we thought... and then Italy did it. And we realized we could." And then they probably reasoned "never let a good crisis go to waste!"*

He was a key person, along with Christian Drosten, in generating alarm during the swine flu "pandemic," which, in hindsight, does look like a dry run for COVID-19. Fortunately, swine flu turned out not to be too infectious. Hundreds of millions worth of vaccines were junked, and fortunately, the population was not vaccinated unnecessarily.

This time around, it's different. Lessons have been learned, and it's full-speed ahead: scare the population into submission, break their will, and vaccinate as many people as possible, ignoring previously established procedures for handling pandemics and, instead, enforcing ineffectual lockdowns, mask-wearing, and the isolation of healthy non-infectious individuals. Bizarrely, large numbers of the population have accepted this, almost without question, which certainly doesn't bode well for the future.

"These days, lockdown feels inevitable. If China had not done it," Neil says, "the year would have been very different."

To those people who, still now, object to lockdowns on civil liberties principles, this will be a chilling reminder of the centrality of the authoritarian Chinese model in influencing global policy in this historic year.

The CDC has mandatory obligations for statistical reporting. Yes, it appears to be a good system, but it's a failing system.

After several years of pursuit to get the release of information from the CDC, USA Today won, revealing that the CDC is among a small group of bio lab operators nationwide that have the worst regulatory histories in the country, receiving repeated sanctions under secretive federal regulations.

Investigations have revealed hundreds of safety incidents at public and private research facilities nationwide and highlighted how many university, government, and private labs have fought to keep records secret about incidents and regulatory sanctions.

It's also been exposed that more than 100 labs working with potential bioterror pathogens have faced secret federal sanctions for safety violations, yet regulators allowed them to keep experimenting while failing inspections, sometimes for years.

The CDC has faced congressional hearings and secret government sanctions over its sloppy lab safety practices and keeping secret large swaths of information about dozens of recent incidents involving some of the world's most dangerous bacteria and viruses in one of the world's most advanced biosafety level 4 labs. There is another Level 4 lab in Wuhan China. There is, of course, no Freedom of Information Act in China, however.

Info obtained thru what wasn't redacted and strings of emails the CDC did not fully check to redact recreated the information above.

Many documents also came from their Medgate Tracking System, which reports on possible outbreaks, biological exposure, accidents, etc.

- After two years to get the info, the CDC needed to cover their tracks of what would be destructive and, of course, what the public blacked out—many details, including the types of viruses and bacteria involved in the mishaps and often the entire descriptions of what actually happened.
- 100 Labs with repeat citations on issues either ignored, deferred, or slowed the process to a stall.
- Regulatory follow-up lacked action, support—regulators just failed to keep up.
- The CDC announces it "strongly recommends" these labs cease all work... but regulators failed to follow up progressively.
- Biologic safety audits were not completed.
- The CDC downplayed extreme high-profile incidents during 2014 with anthrax, Ebola, and a deadly strain of bird flu, later stating it was before new lab safety requirements.
- After losing a box of deadly and highly-regulated influenza specimens, scientists experienced multiple potential exposures involving viruses, bacteria, and safety equipment.
- Boxes from the North Carolina State Laboratory of Public Health were shipped in a re-used box without appropriate packing materials and arrived with a "gaping hole" in one corner, according to the CDC emails. Inside the box were specimens of bacteria that cause potentially life-threatening Typhoid fever.
- Safety records of more than 200 high-containment labs across the nation, facilities whose identities have eluded even the Government Accountability Office were revealed.

- A lab incident from 2013 was also revealed; the agency had been doing controversial work since 2005 using reverse genetics to reconstruct the 1918 flu pandemic virus. CDC refused any info.
- January 6, 2015, USA Today secured 500 pages of CDC documents looking like Swiss cheese—redactions on any incident involving any pathogen that is on a federal list of potential bioterror pathogens, called "select agents."
- CDC lacked key lab incident reporting policy despite scrutiny and promises to improve, Safety experts slammed lax safety practices at CDC labs.
- CDC labs repeatedly faced secret sanctions for mishandling bioterror germs and failing to disclose lab incidents with bioterror pathogens to Congress.

The CDC cited the 2002 bioterrorism law to keep secret the names of government, public and private labs—including its own—that have been suspended or that have faced enforcement actions for violating safety and security regulations in their work with potential bioterror pathogens.

The CDC says they are doing everything to ensure the guidelines for safety are in place. We need more transparency and integrity if we are continuing to have to listen to the narrative from our health authorities and politicians that we just need to "trust the science". That we are learning more each day from the data.

8

The Good, the Bad, the Ugly

"Money does not change hands when someone gets well. Money changes hands when someone gets sick."

—George Orwell

- Obedience To Authority
- The Myth Of Masks
- Cuomo Disaster

Chapter 8

So here we were in early 2020 with professor Neil Ferguson: the man who cried wolf and launched a global first-ever pandemic of fear.

It was his computer model that the politicians around the world listened to kicking off the world's first global pandemic. But the model was off—way off. And now experts say it was "totally unreliable."

The models used to impose these restrictions have been proven to be utterly wrong. According to The Daily Wire, The Imperial College of London model from March showed that as many as 2.2% of Americans could die from COVID-19.

One computer data modeling expert said the Imperial model coding, done by professor Neil Ferguson, is a "buggy mess that looks more like a bowl of angel hair pasta than a finely tuned piece of programming," the Daily Telegraph reported.

"In our commercial reality, we would fire anyone for developing code like this, and any business that relied on it to produce software for sale would likely go bust," David Richards, co-founder of British data technology company WANdisco, told the Telegraph.

What has followed of course is a year and a half and counting-of lockdowns, business destructions and so many controversies from

Government, Science, Health Authorities, and politicians who like many of us, looked like a deer in headlights.

1974 Obedience to Authority: An Experimental View

It didn't take long for the general population to hear the gloom and quickly and quietly move to lockdown. There was a series of social psychology experiments conducted by Yale University psychologist Stanley Milgram on obedience to authority figures. They measured the willingness of study participants, men from a diverse range of occupations with varying levels of education, to obey an authority figure who instructed them to perform acts conflicting with their personal conscience. Participants were led to believe that they were assisting an unrelated experiment, in which they had to administer electric shocks to a "learner." These fake electric shocks gradually increased to levels that would have been fatal had they been real.

The subject is led to believe that for each wrong answer, the learner was receiving actual electric shocks, and shocks that increased with each wrong answer, though in reality there were no such punishments.

Being separated from the subject, the confederate set up a tape recorder integrated with the electro-shock generator, which played pre-recorded sounds for each shock level.

The end result? The majority of people do what they are told to do, irrespective of the content and without conscience. So long as they perceive the command comes from an authority.

This can't be more accurate to what is occurring today. Mainstream media is what the overwhelming majority go to. If some investigate further, they are easily directed to preferable sites to choose from. Why? This is what you would want if you were a Big Tech company, you have the ability to censor.

There have been interviews shared around the world concerning the Whistleblower Dr. Li-Weng Yan. She was a virologist in China (from China) who claimed that COVID-19 was manufactured in a lab, and claimed to have scientific evidence to prove it. She came forward to shed light on the discreet underpinnings of the pandemic in China. Because this story circulated on Facebook, Science Feedback fact-checked it, or attempted to. They rated it as false because her information has not been peer-reviewed.

If a fact-checker rates content as false, it will appear lower in others' news feeds, the Facebook fact-checking page states. This significantly reduces the number of people who see it. Their correction statement was "The virus causing Covid-19 most likely evolved in natural wildlife populations before spreading to humans."

You can really mislead people without outright lying, and in a way, that's more dangerous. You can't prove it false; you can't say what they've said is inaccurate—that it's a lie. You can't say any of that.

Then somebody would have to say it's true—well, it's not true because it's not the whole truth.

The National Center for Health Statistics[22] provides charts and tables that show the types of health conditions and contributing causes mentioned in conjunction with deaths involving coronavirus disease COVID-19. The number of deaths shown for all deaths involving COVID-19 and by age groups. The detailed table breaks down COVID-19, pneumonia, and influenza as of May 16, 2021.

COVID-19 has become the third-leading (underlying) cause of death in the US. Heart disease was 695,000 deaths, Cancer 598,000 and COVID-19 375,000.

The CDC states only 6% of these deaths, COVID-19 was the only cause mentioned on the death certificate. For deaths with conditions or causes in addition to COVID-19 or presumed Covid 19, on average, there were four additional conditions or causes per death.

Definition Of A Real Anti-Vaxxer

First of all, it's a flagrant term used by media and science to categorize anyone, those people who are asking too many questions about vaccines. It's those people who want informed consent and what to spread out the vaccine schedule and or have the choice of what is being mandated to injected into their body or their children. It's mom and dad—all those parents who had a healthy, active, alert, receptive,

[22]https://www.cdc.gov/nchs/nvss/vsrr/covid_weekly/index.htm#Comorbidities

cognitive normal baby, young child, or young teenager until the vaccination. A significant adverse reaction within hours, days, or weeks after the "jab" became a life-changing event. It's those parents who believe it points to one thing as the cause and that is the vaccine. Doctors believe that association is not causation; that the science says vaccines are safe and effective therefore, the vaccine did not cause it.

Eyes Wide Open

What sells now is fear. You don't even know what you don't know. And even if you did know a little it takes an effort to take any action on it. You just listen to mainstream media and obey.

If you're not accessing alternative sources for up-to-date, real information with an array of opinions, then you are in a peg hole of the masses. You are being conditioned by the same narrative from the media. And you refuse to deny it. That you are educated and informed. This is the good work of censorship and deceptive narrative.

The Good, The Bad & The Ugly

The Good: The people of the world have now become aware of events we didn't think could happen. We have learned about what science does know and what they don't know. As humans, it is almost ironic that we can get a virus when science—if you have been paying attention—informs us that we are made up of viruses and bacteria. "What, you mean I have or I am a virus"?

Really, you mean there is a ton of bacteria inside me? Our systems, our gut, our metabolism, and our immune system—sounds like the stock market—is remarkable how it automatically understands foreign bacteria and creates immunity armies to destroy them.

If we have proper sanitation and drinking water and feed our bodies what is meant for us, we will be in great shape. How has the human species survived all this time with millions of viruses everywhere?

What happens when sanitation and clean drinking water come into play? What about our own immune system?

The Bad: The playbook of a pandemic was thrown out the window. Quarantine and protect the vulnerable. We did not protect the vulnerable but lockdowned everyone including 95% of the healthy people. Now a billion dollar campaign to get the dose and moving closer to our youngest of children.

The Ugly: Our advanced healthcare (encompassing all) has already been noted on how the importance of medicine and vaccines. But in between, it has fast-tracked how to leverage you and me for profit. Pharma has changed the rules. Big Tech saw the picture and is now in the pharma and vaccine game. Google and Facebook are basically vaccine companies and control what you say about it.

The desire for power has corrupted the system. How intertwined are the CDC, FDA, and Big Pharma? By Bill Gates's own admission, he will make twenty-fold profit on his investment, well not an investment but philanthropy in vaccines. So $10B will net him $200B.

Follow the science now means follow the narrative. 100 mainstream news channel with the same message almost instantly. The drive to get everyone vaxxed will mean to induce more fear about the evils of a variant. In the UK the Delta variant has been there since April 2021 and now end of July is 90% dominant. But where is the devastation. Extreme downward curve in every category. But the variants will keep the momentum for Pharma. As for the UK and Israel, Health data show the double vaxxed are the majority of new hospitalizations. Hence, the rush for the boosters.

PCR Testing

How reliable was the PCR test for this virus? Well to start with the very person who was the creator of the PCR test was Dr. Kary Mullis, PHD who stated."Anyone can test positive for practically anything with a PCR test if you run it long enough... with PCR if you do it well, you can find almost anything in anybody… it doesn't tell you that you're sick." US health authorities stated early to expect fifty percent false positives.

So here are some facts:

Side Note #1–Viruses come with DNA or RNA genomes. A positive PCR result does not prove the active replication of a virus. It does not prove an infectious virus is present. This is why we prefer to talk about a virus being detected in patients using PCR. Some refer to a PCR positive result as a "viral isolate." Don't. This should be reserved to describe the successful growth of a virus using cell/tissue/organ culture.

In other words, a virus fragment can be picked but is not contagious or infectious.

But today it is perfectly clear that test results are error-prone. How much still cannot be determined due to lack of data? Can you imagine being on the crew ship of Mein Schiff 3 in early 2020 where there was one case that tested positive, which resulted in the lockdown of 2900 people from seventy-three countries into ship quarantine? After testing everyone, only nine positive cases emerged. One person had a cough and the other eight were symptom-free. How is that possible in such a contained environment and people in that specific age group?

Side note #2–We are walking platforms for viruses, bacteria, and fungi.

To science knowledge, "infection" is defined as the proof of an infectious agent AND the proof of multiplication of this agent inside the body (OR associated inflammatory response that can be linked to this agent).

PCR testing is performed in the lab to help us find even tiny amounts of the virus. It does this by amplifying a virus's genetic material to a level where it can be detected.

So many people have little tiny fragments of the virus, which don't represent an infection but are still classified as positive, which meant they have to quarantine and lockdown for fourteen days, then be tested again. This perpetuated the fear as the mountain of cases climbed.

A systematic review shows that there are few epidemiological studies in actual settings. More research is needed to assess the effectiveness of social distancing measures in a variety of industries and work settings. The epidemiological and modeling studies indicate that social distancing in non-healthcare workplaces reduces the overall as well as the peak number of influenza cases. It also delays the influenza peak.

However, for public health measures, another approach is needed. Testing to help slow the spread of SARS-CoV-2 asks not whether someone has RNA in their nose from an earlier infection, but whether they are infectious today. It is a net loss to the health, social, and economic wellbeing of communities if post-infectious individuals test positive and isolate for ten days. Current PCR testing is therefore not the appropriate gold standard for evaluating a SARS-CoV-2 public health test.

Regarding Rapid Test Kits

BMJ. 2021; (published online Jan 12.) From the British Medical Journal, no one questions the need for evidence-based approaches to COVID-19 treatments and vaccines. Why then is this principle being ignored by the governments for testing? In the UK, they also decided to roll out the Innova lateral flow test without supporting evidence, and plan to use it for home use. This of course gives rise to so many more cases. Scientists advised the UK government and the NIH followed suit to change course, as it only leads to fueling the pandemic.

In the face of so much potential for harm and so little evidence of benefit, why would governments who say they listen to the science do this? Because hundreds of millions of Innova testing kits were purchased before it was known how they would perform in people without symptoms and when administered by less than expert hands.

Well, the truth is pretty obvious.

After nine months of research, clinical observation, and accumulated data analysis of millions of people and outcomes worldwide, highly credentialed medical professionals and scientists emphatically disagree. Rational disagreement is often what science requires, especially in the case of COVID-19.

Again, tens of thousands of medical personnel in practice, academia, and research had expressed grave concerns over inconsistencies in diagnoses, data collection, and treatments; flawed diagnostic tools; contradictions in otherwise traditional protocols for peer review and scientific analysis; and a growing compendium of incoherent conclusions. Perhaps this was driven by the need to influence public acceptance of extreme lockdown policies.

Molecular Virology Test

The PCR mold test is done with a swab with little bits of tiny genetic material which goes through a technique amplifying through a series of cycles.

Since the bits of the virus are so tiny, they need to use a technique that will amplify those bits through a series of cycles over and over until there's enough to be detected. If the sample has lots of virus in it, it only requires a few cycles.

What has been happening is that when we test positive, it is interpreted we are infected and infectious to others. But these interpretations have created a problem, as they aren't correct.

Testing positive doesn't mean you have infection. If you are infectious, it requires two things. First that you are shedding the virus found in your droplets. PCR testing absolutely tells us that you are shedding the virus. The second thing is that the virus you are shedding is viable—that it can survive and grow.

The PCR test does not do this. It does not measure infectiousness. So wait. The media counts all positive cases and does not delineate them. It can pick up a non-infectious fragment of the general coronaviruses, which exists in a lot of people, classify it as a case, and ask you to quarantine for two weeks.

What was wrong with this?

The cycle threshold has a relationship if infectiousness or not. At a low cycle threshold, around twenty means there is a high virus load (viral RNA load) and infectious.

At thirty-five to forty cycles, it was found there were only trace amounts and not infectious. So, the problem here is that the results of the test are either positive or negative. Labs have pushed to go to at least forty cycles effectively looking for a Positive before declaring a

Negative. Even Tony Fauci stated the cycles should be around thirty, meaning that if you want to dig deeper, you will find traces of the historic corona family in everyone. PCR tests can pick up bits or fragments of dead virus that were not even infectious, but the test will state positive.

Testing positive doesn't mean you are sick at all or can transmit. So, as it stands, the way we have been using the PCR test has actually been hurting the fight against COVID-19. The public has been made to believe that being tested asymptomatic positive meant for them they were spreaders and needed to isolate.

Finally, the FDA does not allow cycle thresholds (CT) values to be given to public health practitioners, clinics, or the public. What's the sensitivity? It means that a large number of asymptomatic people had a high CT test but were not transmitters. The FDA has a myopic view—lack of intelligent insight causing millions of people to be needlessly quarantined.

Masks

Before 2020, multiple studies on the efficacy of mask-wearing, especially for healthcare workers, had been published by the CDC, *New England Journal of Medicine, Lancet, British Journal of Medicine, Nature, JAMA, PubMed,* and many other professional venues. Nearly all these studies, whether randomized control studies or not, find that mask-wearing to prevent transmission of infectious viruses is inconclusive at best, ineffective at worst. Masks are primarily intended to reduce the emission of virus-laden droplets. That's the science! Some health websites such as few that WHO, CDC, FDA, Health Canada, OSHA (Occupational Safety Health Administration) stated a mask will not prevent or stop a virus.

Overall, most people would agree that it's just plain common sense when you sneeze or cough and you used a tissue, it's going to stop droplets from being released. So, why wouldn't we just believe a mask would do the same thing? Common sense and science would say that it does. It also means that frequently changing your mask. Does it stop a virus? One really needs to listen to the science on this one.

Unfortunately, for many people, no amount of science could convince people that masks are relatively ineffective. The media, the science people, Sanjay Gupta, Tony Fauci, your employer, the stores, and signs everywhere remind us of the importance of masks.

The number one reason for the mandating of masks was to remind you to practice social distancing and wash your hands frequently. The second main reason amounts to behavior modification, and the only political reason for mandating to wear a mask is to enhance and foster fear of the population.

Wearing masks will not make you invincible, and if you are at risk, you should be avoiding high-risk situations like subways and crowded buildings as much as you possibly can most likely a mask will help.

Masks became a symbol—a built-in fear factor for all. In reality, masks act as a logical security blanket, if I wear one I am protected, if you wear one, you are protected. If you don't wear one, you are selfish; you are not listening and obeying the science and therefore deemed a potential super spreader. People panicked when they saw someone without a mask. You don't have to look too far at the media's opportunity to engage on this and portray the grocery store fights and more. On the non-mainstream media venues, you would have seen much more violent police takedowns of someone not wearing a mask in streets absent of people. How extreme! There are videos in so many countries. So on one side people in the US were being subjugated to authority for not wearing a mask among the strict lockdowns and mask-wearing. Yet, thousands of protesters went on for weeks without any discipline on mask-wearing let alone the destruction of businesses and fear in citizens living peaceful lives. Hypocrisy at its best.

People say those that don't wear masks are more likely to get COVID-19 and thus impact our health resources. While that is false, the same could even be said for smokers and their impact on health resources, which is 10-fold higher.

You know the message is working on people who detour around someone walking like it was going to be a head-on collision. But here we are now with the indoctrination of our children preparing them for what–an acceptance of vaccines to come. Putting masks on children is obscene. It is psychologically detrimental to their well-being and that will take its toll in years to come. From Big Pharma's point of view, mission accomplished.

So, here is the orchestrated argument.

Do you think masks work? Are you mask agnostic? Do you wear one because you have to? Do you have anxiety when you see someone not wearing one or it is below the nose. Sounds ridiculous but true. People walking alone in a park, driving alone in their car with a mask—well, they have their reasons, and one of them is certainly fear. F.E.A.R.: False Evidence Appearing Real. If you think they work, then wear one. Don't compel others to wear one.

On Feb 18, 2020, Fauci stated, "This virus is no worse than the flu. Don't worry about it. Be more concerned about influenza, which is going into its second peak, than coronavirus. People don't need to be wearing a mask. It just isn't relevant. You don't need to be wearing a mask and there is a lot of loopholes that let the virus flu." You may think well maybe the world's appointed top spokesperson with credentials didn't know because it was early. If so, you have been fixated on the downplay on the mainstream news. Overall though, the good news about the influenza going into its second peak, is that it appears flu-related hospitalizations and deaths have disappeared. Go figure?

What they say: Data regarding the "real-world" effectiveness of community masking are limited to observational and epidemiological studies. Not random controlled trials RCT. Stopping or lowering droplets has proven to be effective, but stopping viral release has not.

A free and open society can only give the right to individual property rights, and our bodies are our own property. The desire for authoritarians to wield government power, whether through lawfare or brute force, in order to change or mandate others' behavior, whatever the risks for a perceived benefit, is extremely demanding.

The few studies conducted in 2020 on mask-wearing that do endorse the practice concluded mask-wearing may have a positive, correlative, and statistically significant benefit in reducing transmission, especially in preventing transmission from large droplets generated when talking, coughing, sneezing, or spitting. But these conclusions are underscored with authors' acknowledgments that the findings lacked sufficient data to definitively claim that mask-wearing prevents transmission of viruses, cautioning that more research needs to be done.

The gurus of mask-wearing—Occupational Safety and Health—organization that has the science on masks and trains healthcare workers about them…OSHA has remained curiously silent relative to COVID-19 and mask-wearing safety in the workplace, nor has it explained suddenly waiving its safety standards otherwise strictly imposed on employers who require mask/respirator-wearing by employees in the workplace. Mandatory government oversight of this workplace practice confirms there are substantive dangers associated with mask-wearing for prolonged periods, requiring rigorous protocols to mitigate potential health hazards.

1. OSHA strictly regulates the airflow, temperature and humidity, amount of oxygen that must be available throughout the work environment, behind the respirator itself, and in the bloodstream, while wearing respirators. This is especially true in surgery rooms, where the environment is very specifically regulated for optimum oxygen availability, intake, CO2 expulsion, etc.
2. A complete medical evaluation must be completed on each employee required to wear a respirator during work hours to ensure his/her ability to safely wear the device for prolonged periods.
3. Employers must provide a "Respirator Program" for their facilities that meet OSHA requirements for employee safety on penalty of stiff fines, even shutdowns.

So, here is some science. Knowing the differences in approximate sizes of viruses, particles, aerosols, droplets, and mask pores is useful to assess the risks inherent in masks. Viruses are measured in microns, and viruses typically measure.125 microns. Viruses are carried as part of larger particles that range in measurement between 0.02–0.14 microns. Particles are transported in aerosols and droplets. Aerosols are typically less than 5 microns, while droplets are often larger, ranging between 5–10 microns.

Mask pores have a wider range of diameter sizes, anywhere from 80–500 microns. While viruses always travel as part of larger particles carried in aerosols or droplets, mask pores' larger circumference arguably can't prevent most flow through smaller aerosol particles that carry ever-smaller bacteria and viruses.

Why does all this matter? Well, many are firmly against the coercive behavior modification by the certain science/media perspective "based on the inconclusive science currently available, the risks of mandated masking outweigh the perceived rewards."

So, as another piece of the overall puzzle or the agenda here, global citizens have accepted taking off one's shoes and belt, exposing oneself to harmful X-rays, and randomly having your body molested by a stranger in order to get on a commercial airplane flight for safety.

In the above scenario, the government has you over a barrel, so to speak. You need to get on that plane and will suffer the indignities to do so. It started with belts and shoes and now grandma in a wheelchair gets to have a full pat-down.

So, what's next if we quietly and blindly accept, as one submitter put it. "Do us all a favor, and just mask up!"? What's next is mandated vaccinations with risky and dangerous fast-tracked vaccines that you must have. What's next is restrictions on your ability to travel, shop, and bank where you want without an "immunity pass."? Sadly, yes.

Mainstream media is already spouting that succumbing to such draconian measures is patriotic.

Sars had a 15% mortality rate but within a year it disappeared. Yet here we are with one-quarter of one percent lethality for this disease is non-compelling justification for the lockdowns or healthy people to wear masks to protect others when 99.75% of those who contract COVID will not perish and further the majority of those who will die from COVID have 2 or more comorbidity complications and in an older age group. This is a perverse policy that threatens psychological damage from a constant manufactured message of fear of others, and of the environment, evidenced by an ever-masked population.

A violation of each individual's natural right to control his/her own body and the risks that accrue.

The lack of an iron-clad, unambiguous, and uncontroversial justification before any government/health authority is permitted a scintilla of jurisdiction over our livelihoods, our natural rights to live, survive, and thrive as a response to any public threat.

Look no more than to NY's Governor Cuomo who received letters of complaint from his condo management of his continued refusal to wear a mask in elevators and areas. Then, photos in public without a mask. Then he pushes for mandatory masks stating " masks are good, masks are cool and becoming a part of cultural communication. If I could sign an executive order to say it's cool, I would."

Cuomo

What was identified early with this virus from China and Italy was that there was one group that really needed to be protected from COVID-19 in the group over sixty-five with co-morbidity. And people in long-term care homes. This was already well known from experiences with other viruses H1N1, Mers, and Sars.

A March 25 decision by NY Governor Andrew Cuomo was a Health Department directive that required nursing homes to take recovering coronavirus patients. More than 9,000 recovering coronavirus patients in New York state were released from hospitals into nursing homes early in the pandemic under a controversial directive. Cuomo administration has been forced in recent weeks to acknowledge it has been underreporting the overall number of COVID-19 deaths among long-term care residents. It is now nearly 15,000 up from what was previously disclosed. Because he has attempted to hide the data the FBI has an investigation.

Instead of protecting this vulnerable group, Cuomo had COVID-19 patients return to their retirement homes. These retirees ended up being totally isolated in their rooms and infecting others. This also happened in other states but not on the scale as New York. This is the wisdom of government with no common sense and either being misguided by science or ignoring it.

Cuomo Brothers

The coronavirus blame game continues from New York Governor Andrew Cuomo.

It's no secret that states with Democrat governors have had the most coronavirus deaths per capita, the majority of the George Floyd protests, and the slowest economic recoveries—and don't expect them to take the blame for it.

In March 2020, before it became politically convenient to say otherwise, Cuomo praised Trump for the federal government's role in helping his state during the crisis. "His team is on it. They've been responsive. I want to say thank you," he said at a press conference in March. "He has delivered for New York. He has," Cuomo said of President Trump. In May, Cuomo credited President Trump's help with preventing an extra 100,000 people from being hospitalized with the virus.

But the tables soon changed with how Cuomo responded to the coronavirus. It was an unmitigated disaster that they botched despite all the help they received. It was then quite convenient to divert blame away from himself and went on the attack, claiming Trump was responsible for every single COVID-19-related death in the Empire State.

Cuomo was chastising Trump for not banning travel from Europe until mid-March, but on March 19 Cuomo was telling the public that "fear and panic" are just as big a problem as the coronavirus.

The Cuomo brothers became a frequent tag team to watch on CNN, as they often exchanged family jabs on live TV calling each other on family matters along with all the pharma sponsored advertising in between, and then showing concern for the tough times they were in.

Governor Cuomo made a colossal error of judgment. In fact, it wasn't a case of bad judgment. It was his own personal agenda to showcase himself, how bad it was (supposed to be) in New York—how bad it was and how to turn it into a political rally.

There was one Republican County Executive of Rensselaer County who rightly saw Cuomo's order as absurd and defied it. This was the only nursing home run by the county, and Van Rensselaer Manor saw a total of zero coronavirus deaths.

Now, the NY Times are ripping him for denying it ever happened, as he claims that his nursing home policy actually never existed at all and now the FBI investigation After that, the Cuomo brothers' reunions on CNN kind of disappeared. And so did any reporting from CNN. What a surprise!

There never has been a question of the political play here trying to make every opportunity for political points work.

Despite undergoing the most severe lockdowns, states run by Democrat Governors accounted for the majority of the nation's coronavirus deaths. Disastrous policies on nursing homes in those blue states are among the primary culprits for the discrepancy. In late 2020, Of the ten states with the lowest unemployment rates, nine are led by Republican governors. The inverse is true of the ten states with the highest unemployment rates, nine of which are run by Democrat governors.

How is it possible that anyone with common sense—he obviously didn't have any—didn't care or didn't ask about the science of the impact of these actions? How could anyone do this? Now if we step back for a moment and think about the big picture from countries around the world, how health authorities stepped in, politicians being put in a trance or others found an opportunity to yield power and so many making decisions on lockdowns with rules for some and not others. Common sense went out the window–and really, some of the science too.

9

Censorship—The Narrative Becomes Believable

"The man who reads nothing at all is better educated than the man who reads nothing but newspapers."

—Thomas Jefferson

- Pharma Has New Partners
- Two Sides Of Facebook
- Bad Omen For Democracy

Chapter 9

Google Becoming A Vaccine Company

Why have Google and Facebook become so extremely engaged in censoring and organizing your searches for you via their algorithms?

Why has Google become a vaccine company, now with a partnership with Glaxo? Google is also making vaccines and they're partnered with Merck, and they're shutting down discussions about what they call "vaccine misinformation" that is not misinformation at all.

YouTube's owner, Google, is effectively a vaccine company. Two subsidiaries of Google's parent company, Alphabet, market and manufacture vaccines: Calico and Verily. Arthur Levinson, Genentech's former CEO, runs Calico, an anti-aging drug company, while Verily teams up with Big Pharma to conduct drug and vaccine clinical trials.

In 2016, Alphabet inked a $715 million deal with GlaxoSmithKline to create and develop bioelectronic medicines and vaccines and to mine medical information from Google customers. Google's Customer Services President, Mary Ellen Coe, sits on Merck's board.

In 2016, Google partnered with Sanofi launching Onduo, a virtual diabetes clinic, and in 2018 in another business that uses analytics to develop new drugs and vaccines. The pair will also deploy artificial intelligence to help forecast sales and optimize marketing.

In 2018, Google invested $27,000,000 in Vaccitech to make vaccines for flu, MERS, and prostate cancer. Vaccitech calls itself "the future of mass vaccine production." Well, that's frightening!

In 2020, Vaccitech started work on a COVID vaccine. Google claims to provide politically and commercially neutral searches, but it systemically manipulates search results to suppress accurate vaccine safety and efficacy information and steers users toward deceptive and fraudulent Pharma propaganda.

Google's algorithms censor negative information about COVID vaccines and positive information about therapies like hydroxychloroquine that compete with the vaccines in development. Google censors reports that diminish public panic about COVID-19. Google's definition of "misinformation" is "any information, even if accurate and true, which criticizes vaccination products." Facebook and Google hired "FactChecker" (Politifact) to censor vaccine misinformation.

Politifact was launched by a grant from the Gates Foundation, the world's largest vaccine promoter. Google's orchestrated censorship across social media is crippling legitimate debates over international vaccination policies. This is a crisis for liberal democracies.

Bill Gates is on the highway to the globe riding the wave with pharma to roll out more vaccines and Big Tech has seen the huge global opportunity. It's a large pie, and there's a lucrative piece for all of them. Pharma's power and position are already well-established, with Bill Gates funding the infrastructure—the WHO, GAVI, the studies, the grants, medical journalism, and his investments in vaccines. Then, Big Tech behind the helm with all the technology controls to make it happen.

Big tech has openly admitted that they are going to censor anyone who questions the safety of vaccines, or even hints that we should have better safety monitoring systems even though VAERS.

Zach Vorhies, the whistleblower who was a software engineer for Google, stated that Google, in the past three years, has rolled out changes that purposely down-rank independent health websites, even extremely high-quality and independent medical articles that are written by credentialed healthcare professionals.

Google removed many of the top natural health and health freedom websites from their organic search results, with some of them losing as much as 99% of their traffic.

The censorship that is being applied to alternative health, therapeutics like Remdisvir, HydroxyC, Ivermectin, and the merits of Vitamin D and Zinc that some clinics have used with success are being suppressed.

I personally experienced Google controlling some of my searches about vaccine controversies. General searches normally present a million-plus results. About 90% of users don't look past the first page or do another search. When I needed to drill down to find facts, I used a Boolean search. This is a query methodology that is used to broaden, narrow, or refine search results bringing results down and better criteria to the front pages but still getting a few hundred thousand returns. Regardless, Google refined my search selecting just 164 returns and a notification: "In order to help with your searches, we provided you with this selection (not those words exactly)." should I wish to try another search, I could. I reviewed the pages Google selected for me and the topics were mostly *opposite* about my topic search on vaccine controversies.

The Strategy Against Anti-Vaxxers

In January 2019, the WHO announced that vaccine hesitancy was one of the ten greatest threats to the planet. Of course, it seems to follow the vaccine agenda.

The pharmaceutical industries help dictate that message. In March 2019, Democrat Adam Schiff wrote to Mark Zuckerberg asking for the removal of any information/misinformation that was against safe and effective vaccines.

Who Is Funding The Covert Censorship Group?

Influence Watch, which monitors individuals and groups that influence public policy, describes the Center for Countering Digital Hate—CCDH—as a "London-based advocacy group that targets accused 'hate groups' and individuals for de-platforming campaigns to remove them from major social media outlets" and "has ties to the left-wing British Labor Party and British left-progressivism." The anonymously funded CCDH also has an office in Washington, DC, and the defamatory publicity campaign created in December 2020 was designed to discredit the National Vaccine Information Center[23] founded by dissatisfied parents. NVIC's four-decade public record of working within the US democratic system to secure vaccine safety and informed consent protections in public health policies and laws, all their work was being attacked.

Facebook

The world of US media and Democrats completely flipped out when Trump won. Throughout the whole campaign, he was attacked, talk shows ridiculed him, and propaganda flourished everywhere. Facebook was all in to influence, and they did. Also, in the allowance of which ads on the platform, it was China, Russia, and FB against Trump. Facebook has been hit with a long list of fines such as 'false or misleading representations' about users' privacy. But the largest one was with Cambridge Analytics. Congressional hearings and watchdog groups found that they had access to 50 million profiles and used them to target ads during the 2016 presidential election campaign.

At the time, Facebook said it knew the firm had violated its policies by obtaining and secretly passing on the data, which users had agreed to share with a personality prediction app. There were given a $5 billion fine and their stock price went up. So, this is the trusted Big Tech who is fact-checking, putting on a notice stating false, removing, and or blocking your account based on vaccine info you posted from

[23]https://www.nvic.org

the WHO or CDC that is a trusted source. And we are supposed to believe Facebook.

But these are only the starting points. And yet you still use Facebook being influenced without you knowing–or at best you don't care.

Facebook users are seeing more targeted ads from pharmaceutical companies—an ethical gray area for patient data and privacy, the Washington Post reports.

Why it matters: Drug companies don't need to know your medical history to target you for a drug, and seeing a surprisingly relevant medical ad can feel invasive.

How it works: Drug companies can use your browsing history, along with your age, gender, and location, to figure out health issues you may have and market their treatment.

By the numbers: Pharmaceutical and health care brands spent nearly $1 billion last year on Facebook mobile ads. Their spending has nearly tripled over two years, according to Pathmatics, an advertising analytics company. Do you think they have influence?

Health privacy laws like HIPAA don't address this intersection of drug companies, data brokers, and social media networks.

It's not just Google either—Amazon, IBM, and Microsoft have also struck deals with hospitals across the country to gain access to patient data, the Wall Street Journal reports.

Why it matters: it reveals just how expansive the relationship between tech companies and hospitals has become—and lawmakers have taken notice.

Unfortunately, there's no evidence of wrongdoing; hospitals can share patient data as long as they follow federal law.

The deals have the potential to yield information and products valuable to patients. For example, Microsoft is partnering with Providence, a large hospital system, to create oncology algorithms using doctor's notes in medical records.

The *Wall Street Journal* writes:

> *"Digitizing patients' medical histories, laboratory results and diagnoses has created a booming market in which tech giants are looking to store and crunch data, with potential for groundbreaking discoveries and lucrative products."*

So, Facebook was caught illegally harvesting biometric data. along with facial recognition of patient.

Facebook ended up agreeing to pay a negotiated $550 million to settle a 2015 class-action privacy lawsuit against its use of facial recognition technology.

From a business perspective, you can see how Facebook might see pushing vaccine product lines upon ill-informed populations as low-hanging fruit for easy profits. During Zuckerberg's testimony to Congress: Congressman Posey: Well, how do you discourage access or postings on anti-vaccine information?

Zuckerberg: "Well, there are a number of different tactics. For example, if someone is typing into the search results, into the search box, something that might lead to anti-vaxx content, we don't recommend anti-vaxx searches to them."

This is the second major settlement from Facebook in six months, after a huge $5 billion settlement with the US FTC last year over users' privacy violations.

If you compare vaccine product lines, pharmaceutical drugs, and medical devices. The latter two have several disadvantages:

- Lengthy testing required, and pre-licensure approval times on the front end to get the products to the market
- Legal liability for harm caused on the backend
- PR nightmares via legal liabilities

Vaccines have none of those issues. Vaccine products come with reassurance from both Big Tech and corporate media that criticism or talk of harm caused by the products will be censored. Vaccine manufacturers are fully indemnified. Laws across America are racing to mandate all vaccine product lines on children and adults while removing any barrier to such ends—including parent intervention.

The WHO has stated that they want to harmonize the registered databases and track each individual's immunization status, leveraging immunization registries, electronic databases, and national identification number systems.

It's looking like a reality TV show—The Amazing Race where all the Big Pharma companies fueled by Bill Gates investments vie for their share of global vaccinations.

Our God-given immune system is extremely complex and has evolved since the beginning of time to eliminate threats. It has so many components that all must work together, it's like a beautiful symphony, and no one on this planet fully understands how the music is played. It is the height of arrogance and foolishness to think that nature's perfect symphony can be improved by injecting into the body a man-made cocktail of viral DNA/RNA fragments, aborted fetal cells, monkey kidney tissue, egg albumin, heavy metals, mercury, formaldehyde, MSG, Polysorbate 80, and myriad other toxic adjuvants.

It's hard to do, because of all the censorship and suppression of information going on, but people can still find the truth about vaccines if they want to know it.

In fact, there is suppressed information that shows some vaccines weaken immunity and increase the likelihood of catching seasonal flus and colds. Vaccines can also confuse the immune system and greatly increase the incidence of autoimmune conditions and they increase the potential for a deadly "cytokine storm" response to a viral infection.

Since the National Childhood Vaccine[24] Act of 1986, manufactures of vaccines have had total immunity from liability for any injuries or deaths caused by vaccines. If vaccines are so safe and effective, why did the corrupt Big Pharma lobbyists buy the politicians to push through this legislation? If they are immune from liability, what incentive do vaccine manufactures have to develop safe vaccines? Follow the money. The global vaccine market was $47 billion in 2019 and projected to more than double in the next 5 years. Vaccines have become one of the biggest frauds ever in terms of their desire for profit and the Covid vaccines might be the biggest one ever.

The practice of reporting only facts and opinions that comply with official narratives has long been de rigueur in electronic media outlets dependent on Big Pharma advertising revenue.

It's a bad omen for democracy when citizens can no longer conduct civil, informed debates about critical policies that impact the vitality

[24]https://www.hrsa.gov/vaccine-compensation

of our economy, public health, personal freedoms, and constitutional rights. Censorship is violence, and this systematic muzzling of debate that proponents justify as a measure to curtail dangerous polarization is actually fueling those divisions. All our advances in science are the results of science challenging questions and debates to prove that a hypothesis can be proven or not. The science people connected with the Covid-19 agenda are not listening to the 43 thousand medical practitioners who are against what is happening.

Edward R. Murrow's warning that: "The right to dissent... is surely fundamental to the existence of a democratic society. That's the right that went first in every nation that stumbled down the trail to totalitarianism."

As Murrow predicted, the imposition of censorship has masked the systematic demolition of our Constitution, including attacks on freedom of worship (including abolishing religious exemptions and closing churches), freedom of assembly, private property (the right to operate a business), due process (including the imposition of far-reaching restrictions against freedom of movement, education, association with notice, and comment rulemaking) and the 7th amendment right to jury trials (in cases of vaccine injuries caused by corporate negligence).

By James Grundvig, Vaxxter Contributor and Investigative Reporter:

On one edge, Big Pharma clouds the truth with disinformation and labels those inquiring about problems associated with as "anti-vaxxers." On the other edge, vaccine manufacturers have created funnels taking their point of view to the top of Facebook search results. Google changed its algorithms to push the CDC and World Health Organization (WHO) articles to the top of the first page while burying alternative views.

On December 10, YouTube has enforced its new terms of service, which will allow the company to delete any account it deems to be "not commercially viable." Facebook took a more blatant censorship approach earlier this year.

When users search for vaccine risk information, they are redirected to a CDC or WHO web page. Facebook has also created pop-up warnings to censor sites that post vaccine information that it deems to be is contrary to pro-vaccine dogma.

Naturally, Big Pharma deploys other tools to place muzzles on what it believes are inquisitors and anti-vax insurgents. Pharma controls mainstream media and TV news narratives with oceans of advertising dollars. Pharma pays medical experts to make sure their mainstream views are primary and reportedly hires internet trolls to delete posts written in the comments section of articles and blogs that challenge distorted, one-sided information that disparages vaccine activists who challenge pro-vaccine dogma.

Some other of Pharma's hardball tactics:

- Holding focus groups and using the information to help write healthcare and vaccine bills for bought politicians at both the state and federal levels.
- Lobbying all elected officials at the state and federal levels, spending more than $1B each year to buy the results they are seeking.
- Influencing advisory committees of the captured agencies, such as the CDC and FDA.
- Holding pediatricians' hostage by paying a bonus of $400 per child if 63% of the children in their practice have been fully vaccinated by two years of age with all doses of the 10 vaccines in the pediatric schedule.

Unless vaccine reactions impact a person or a member of their family directly, most Americans have no idea they were stripped of their right to informed consent. With their injury, they became a cog in the global vaccine agenda: to create customers for life for pharma. Parents say some of those side effects include ADD, ADHD, asthma, allergies, eczema, seizure disorders, autoimmune diseases, narcolepsy, primary ovarian failure, Guillain Barre Syndrome.

What can people do to counter the billions of dollars pharma uses to market, lobby, influence, and buy off the news media, medical associations, and doctors?

10

The Play

"All the world's a stage and most of us are desperately unrehearsed."

—Seán O'Casey

- The Stage Is Set
- Passports Or Segregation
- Barrington And Civil Rights

Chapter 10

Act 1 of a theatre production. Government, Big Pharma, and COVID-19 are a few of the main actors stumbling out from behind the curtain, flip-flopping dialogue, hypocritical statements creating mass confusion, stating listen to the science all while evil actors keep you from seeing what the real plot is behind the scenes keeping all your eyes glued to the narrative.

The global audience finds themselves in the longest-running play ever, captivated by fear and a willingness to do anything to leave the theatre back to the real world. One that no one has experienced before in a seemingly surreal situation as if we are all on stage, part of the act we cannot escape from.

The plot continues to build, luring the audience into a sense of security. (Other supporting characters Astra, Pfizer, Moderna, and Johnson & Johnson are in the background, working the ropes and pulleys.)

The second act has an uplifting effect. If the audience just listens to the story and takes on the new way of life, takes an experimental elixir, and enjoys The Great Reset the main characters will fade away but always be there to protect you and maybe the play will end. Most of the audience knows there has been and will be a huge cost but has become complacent, indoctrinated to the narrative of the play.

The audience feels like they have heard and seen the same play every day for almost 2 years and feel that if they just give in to what the cast wants, they'll be free. But the play doesn't end and Act 3 and 4 has massaged your willpower to resist, to do what pseudoscience, the global elite and the collaborative cast of characters have in store for you. Some of the audience believed there was only one way out but will become a false premise. Ask why. Demand answers. Question every cast member their role. The truth is out there. Look at alternative venues–like another play–but its truth has been censored. The audience needs to take back their freedom and rights otherwise, they will be trapped without rights in a never-ending story.

Immunity Passports–A New Journey To Inequality

Immunity passports, vaccine certificates, and digital tracking were really years away, but Covid-19 has provided the opportunity for what governments and the global elite have been waiting for—surveillance. can continue then the new strains, the new variants will keep the momentum supported. Because there are so many unknowns, the whole thing could backfire in the short term, but it won't disappear. This is an opportunity for the advancement of mass surveillance.

The ability to be "safer"—to return to work or move through society more freely. It follows that those without these passports would be afforded less freedom.

Denying people access to employment or other opportunities, based on a medical record. For a government to rob people of a constitutional right (liberty) based on a justification that amounts to an unproven hypothesis (antibody passport) is the definition of unconstitutional.

Yet, that's not the worst problem.

The worst problem is the dangerous legal categorization of human beings: safe, unsafe, at risk, other. We know what happens when we create social systems dividing people into categories—abuse, discrimination, and oppression.

Such an outcome becomes increasingly likely with every new social privilege that relies on having a passport showing you are a "safe" human: so, if jobs depend on it, if education depends on it, if access to social necessities like grocery stores depend on it, and if the ability to travel depends on it, we're in dire straits.

The key is privacy. The system is predicated on the idea that we should be sharing particular kinds of health information about ourselves widely. That shouldn't be a given; health information has long been understood as one of the most sensitive, personal categories of information. If governments mandated the sharing of health information, it may not survive judicial review because the science is so shaky.

However, what makes this so dangerous is that governments need not mandate its use. By calling it optional—a deceptive narrative—the idea sounds like it respects privacy, when in fact, that consequence of not getting a passport makes it far from consensual.

For an immunity passport system to work, there will have to be a new surveillance infrastructure to facilitate the collection and sharing of this personal health information.

Rules surrounding who collects the data and who gets to use it might start out narrowly, with privacy in mind, but the risk that over time those rules will loosen and shift is real.

> *"We do not encourage at this stage that getting a vaccination determines whether you can travel internationally or not."*
>
> —Hans Kluge, WHO Europe

The Common Trust Network and the World Economic Forum have partnered with several airlines including Cathay Pacific, JetBlue, Lufthansa, Swiss Airlines, United Airlines, and Virgin Atlantic, as well as hundreds of health systems across the United States and the government of Aruba.

The CommonPass app created by the group allows users to upload medical data such as a Covid-19 test result or, eventually, a proof of vaccination by a hospital or medical professional, generating a health certificate or pass in the form of a QR code that can be shown to authorities without revealing sensitive information. For travel, the app lists health pass requirements at the points of departure and arrival based on your itinerary.

Digital Health Pass IBM (IBM) developed its own app, called Digital Health Pass, which allows companies and venues to customize indicators they would require for entry, including coronavirus tests, temperature checks, and vaccination records

In 2018, West Virginia teachers went on strike when they were mandated to wear FitBits to monitor their activities to determine the insurance premiums for their medical coverage.

In France, factory workers were being made to wear devices that beep when they come within six feet of another worker as if they are cattle.

In Michigan US, there is a bill called the Microchip Protection Act, which is said to prevent employers from requiring a sub-dermal microchip implant for employees to keep their job.

August 17, 2020, Ontario Government Agrees To Human Rights Groups' Demands To End Police Access To Covid Database

A Freedom movement legal challenge against the Ontario government has ended police access to a COVID-19 database to stop the blanket disclosure of personal medical information for law enforcement. Ontario police had been accessed the testing results database over 95,000 times, reviewing personal health information. They didn't have this access before but someone decided without good justification, that it would help them do their jobs more safely.

Surveillance

Governments across the world are have been availing every surveillance tool at their disposal to help stem the spread of the novel coronavirus, using our smartphones. And Governments are also receiving support from private tech companies.

A live index of ramped-up security measures by Top10VPN.com details the countries that have already brought in measures to track the phones of coronavirus patients, ranging from anonymized aggregated data to monitor the movement of people more generally, to the tracking of individuals (suspected patients and their contacts), known as contact tracing.

Samuel Woodhams, Top10VPN's Digital Rights Lead who compiled the index, warned that the world could slide into permanently increased surveillance.

"Without adequate tracking, there is a danger that these new, often highly invasive, measures will become the norm around the world," he told Business Insider. "Although some may appear entirely legitimate, many pose a risk to citizens' right to privacy and freedom of expression."

Countries

The tracking data that goes into the map isn't limited to mobile phone data or credit card records. Face-to-face interviews with patients are even being used to build a retroactive map of where they've been.

South Korea is using messages warning people they may have come into contact with someone carrying the virus.

Electronic wristbands on those who ignore home-quarantine orders. A refusal to use the band would result in the person being moved to a shelter.

In Canada, completely voluntary data is anonymized (or de-identified) on secure servers. But re-identifying can be done if data is not deleted or hacked. Drones are monitoring in Australia.

Israel passed new laws to spy on its citizens' March 17, and Israel's Security Agency will no longer have to obtain a court order to track individuals' phones.

Taiwan has activated what it calls an "electronic fence," which creates alerts on quarantined people leaving the house.

Having your phone turned off means they have lost they lost track of you and warrants a police visit.

Poland created an app called "Home Quarantine" and uses it to make people send geo-located selfies when requested. Failure to comply within twenty minutes results in a police visit. Belgium is using anonymized data from telcos. Similar to Canada, Italy has created movement maps.

The Indian government has launched a smartphone app called "AarogyaSetu Aadhaar" (English: foundation or base), a unique twelve-digit identity number that can be obtained voluntarily by residents or passport holders of India, based on their biometric and demographic data. Aadhaar is now the world's largest biometric ID system.

China Leads The Way

Wuhan was the test location for 30k 5G towers, and now it has fully rolled out its controversial social credit score. Under the system, both financial behaviors like "frivolous spending" and bad behaviors like lighting up in smoke-free zones can result in stiff consequences.

Penalties include loss of employment and educational opportunities, as well as transportation restrictions. It's the largest surveillance system in the world and is expected to roll out six hundred million cameras in the next two years—along with the backbone of 5G.

Civil Rights Violation

Currently, people generate codes in Alipay and WeChat, which are mega-apps in China that nearly every citizen has installed on their phones and that they use to do everything from chatting to buying basic goods to hailing rides.

Some of these measures impose severe restrictions on people's freedoms, including their privacy and other human rights. Unprecedented levels of surveillance, data exploitation, and misinformation are being tested across the world.

"It really is an extraordinary invasion of privacy for a democratic state to request," said Brenda McPhail, the director of the Canadian Civil Liberties Association's privacy, technology and surveillance project.

Children's Health Defense (CHD) is a non-profit watchdog group that roots out corruption in federal agencies, including the Centers for Disease Control and Prevention (CDC), the World Health Organization (WHO), and the Federal Communications Commission (FCC), and exposes wrongdoings in the pharmaceutical and telecom industries.

Use of ankle bracelets to track citizens who flout lockdown rules. Ai cameras that track social distancing and mask-wearing in the workplace. The list goes on and on.

Since the outbreak of COVID-19, governments around the world have implemented a wide range of digital tracking measures, developed dozens of contact tracing apps, and introduced new physical surveillance initiatives in a bid to slow the spread of the virus.

While some of these may well be necessary and legitimate during these unprecedented times, some have dramatically threatened citizens' civil liberties and right to privacy.

COVID-19 Digital Rights Data Trackers

A Live Index: https://www.top10vpn.com/research/%20covid-19-digital-rights-tracker

Key Findings:

- There are currently seventy-three digital health certificate apps in operation.
- They have been downloaded at least 18.8 million times combined.
- Sixty apps (82%) have inadequate privacy policies.
- US developers have created almost half (thirty-five) of all apps
- Employee screening apps (nineteen) and venue access apps (nineteen) are the most common, followed by international travel apps (seventeen).

Digital health certificates are yet another example of developers, private companies, and governments attempting to solve a complex public health crisis with rushed and poorly designed technology.

Barrington Declaration

We have 50,000 scientists and world-renowned virologists and doctors across the globe that have signed on to the Great Barrington Declaration, stating that this COVID pandemic has been mishandled;

there should have been no masks except for those that are very susceptible—that being 0.4% of the population. That's right: 0.4% is what this has all been about. 0.4 are at high risk. 99.6% of the population of the world experience what would be described as mild symptoms.

Interestingly, for all the recommendations to protect the vulnerable in the Great Barrington Declaration, nowhere does it mention the masks (widespread use), testing (other than for nursing home staffs), or contact tracing.

The so-called "great reset" promises to build "a more secure, more equal, and more stable world" if everyone on the planet agrees to "act jointly and swiftly to revamp all aspects of our societies and economies, from education to social contracts and working conditions."

But it wouldn't have been possible to contemplate materializing such an all-encompassing plan for a new world order without a global crisis, be it manufactured or of unfortunate happenstance, that shocked society to its core.

11

The Impact of Lockdown

"Injustice anywhere is a threat to justice everywhere."

—Martin Luther King Jr

- War on Covid or You
- Pandemic playbook rules rewritten overnight
- Life Impact 100 fold greater than Covid

Chapter 11

Has this been the biggest political blunder ever? It really only depends on how it has impacted you, frontline workers, your community, and the action of communities and countries around the world. Further, now you should be aware of how quickly your rights and freedom can be taken despite a Constitution or Charter of Rights.

If you didn't have 'Eyes Wide Open,' then you missed a lot. What we've seen are fear-driven—not science-driven—decisions advocated by leaders who have the power to use executive powers and did so. On the streets, there were thousands of scenes everywhere of police takedowns on anyone—any age—who defied any rule. If your eyes were just open, then you listened only to mainstream media. Remote control to twenty different news stations, and the narrative is identical. Media has the highest ratings ever by sensationalizing daily cases and deaths knowing that keeping the fear level puts ratings through the roof.

Science slowly took the opportunity to be recognized and pull legitimate strings, but other (absurd) positions were embellished to keep their agendas in front. Doctors and all the specialists who want to speak out risk losing all they have studied and worked for even if they are correct. There were, however, many that did.

As the World Economic ForumWEF states on their website: “You will own nothing and be happy”

To those who believe and hold on to the false belief that “but we saved lives” on lockdown, you obviously have taken no initiative to uncover the simple truth.

The consequence of a pandemic is, indeed, preparedness. We learned from Sars that the vulnerable must be protected. We know that people with co-morbidity health issues need protection. This was not done.

We shut down society thinking that we can and will protect all. The fear is what has pushed this forward by the media and their experts.

The management of COVID-19 infection including all the PPE, PCR & tracking as medically valuable as they may be, but risk stripping citizens of privacy; becoming a different version of the New World Order, in which people’s antibodies or immunities will or will not allow them to work or to travel.

Illness in our modern era has usually been private. Until now, we never needed to disclose not-obvious illnesses to our neighbors, let alone to the government. That is one reason we can have the level of privacy that has been ours. The commons could no longer kill us. My infection did not kill you; yours did not kill me.

But with COVID-19, illness can be framed as a public matter and certainly, one that gives the government a central role, and thus a high status and a great deal of authority in managing our bodies. Our temperatures being taken in front of strangers in a store or at work to announcements of the infections of public figures on social media, COVID’s lethality is being used to explain why, whether we are sick or well, we should all abandon any expectations of privacy and autonomy. Effectively, we all have been told to walk around and behave as if we are infected. We are all positioned as hypothetically ill and continually told that we should act as if we are all “potentially infected.”

It also means that we are thus all expected, whether sick or perfectly healthy, to release our rights to privacy and autonomy.

The downside of this is well beyond its potential medical value. Is it going to create a public category of second-class citizens whose bodies determine their potential in life? And depending on what we do or don't have in our bodies, it can be revealed on any track and trace database, or our antibodies, or the records of our medical treatment.

It seems that all of this is the foundation of what is to come and seemingly one step away. Limited options for non-compliance. Your job opportunities, schooling, travel, and general freedoms may be going, going gone. The government will dictate what they and the science believe should be in our bodies.

It's important that we not be misled whatever national policies our leaders create in this pandemic and know that this is not just some drastic social experiment being tried on a global scale.

Will lockdown and quarantine solve the problem of COVID-19 infections? Medically, it helps to contain the pandemic, but we should not part with the basic human rights and demands of a free society. We really should not be afraid to ask: how long and with what severity, based on what data, tolerating what intrusions and tracking of the body, and at what other set of costs?

What exactly is the exit strategy with COVID-19?

We realized this would be a long, dragged-out crisis and that it would probably/inevitably involve shortages in the supply chain, mass unemployment, rent-based evictions, the death of small businesses, chaos in the cities, misery everywhere, and that as always in emergencies and what amounted to a war footing, though the enemy was a virus, some people had more and earlier knowledge of its dimensions than others.

Will the COVID-19 "lockdown" entail expectations—that are now becoming habits, that are soon to become lifestyles, then memories, to the point where our kids won't remember life before this? Will it guarantee to keep people from engaging in the kinds of behavior that survivors of war require: solidarity, love, new encounters, private communications, and hugs?

Has it become a real pandemic? They often begin with fake policy. And this one has.

So, when you read that ten billionaires have made more billions than before out of their previous billions in the pandemic... is that opportunity? Was it because small businesses, which represent more revenue, taxes, and our economic foundation, were basically crippled due to government intervention?

Amazon, Walmart, and Costco, of course, were companies that were considered essential. UK Prime Minister Boris Johnson contracted to them to manage COVID-19 data from the NHS. Palantir (owned by far right-wing Peter Thiel), Google, and Microsoft gave the COVID-19 data management contracts;

In the US, Health and Human Services (HHS) gave their COVID-19 contracts to the same entities. Stef Simanowitz of Amnesty UK broke this story, one of the biggest stories of this century, and to date, no mainstream media have picked it up yet.

What does that mean—that the contracts for managing COVID-19 data of NHS, HHS have gone to these tech giants? So much for data privacy with their track record of privacy breaches. The test swabs with your DNA info are supposed to be destroyed within six weeks. Are they?

It means that it is not really in my, your, or government officials' hands to control. The control, the information, and the statistics that would be fed to the Ministry of Health department worldwide and then to the government explaining they are listening to the data—the science.

Our wellbeing, our ability to plan for our own health, our ability to go back into the world of sunlight, our ability to see human faces, our ability to embrace our elderly relatives, go back to school, and have town meetings is not in the hands of actual medical doctors at government agencies or even in the hands of our elected government officials.

With big tech in control, having vested interests in their enrollment of vaccines (having created vaccine companies), they can dial the data up or down. It then can be taken further to the investment world where it's possible they can hedge, short, or invest in economies that they can dial up or down. Sort of like legal insider trading—forever.

Let's go one step further. If Google decides what news about COVID-19 you see or search for while Facebook also censors/manages news about COVID-19), and if Palantir creates the millions of bots (spam) regarding COVID-19 on social media, you will be told any story they want about where we are with the COVID-19 pandemic, the variants (or the next pandemic... and the next one).

This means we can't trust the COVID-19 data presented on even very official-looking platforms—even platforms with government insignias—in order to make our decisions about something as basic as going back to school, because the official-looking websites are thoroughly corrupted already... by the profit motive.

Is This The War On Covid-19 Or, Rather, The War On You?

1000 medical doctors wrote to Donald Trump at the end of May 8, 2020, stating that there will be millions of casualties in plain sight but they will be called suicides, alcoholism, heart attack, and luminous depression. And in youth, it will be called financial instability, unemployment, higher drug use, despair, unplanned pregnancy, poverty, abuse, and suicide. This expression was pleading to governments, explaining that taking extreme measures can be worse than the pathogen itself.

- The emergency powers taken by the Government have been abused—they were not designed to be used over such a long period of time.
- The "Napoleonic" principle that everything is illegal unless you are explicitly allowed is an inversion of the way the law has worked in this country throughout modern times. If you had told a human rights expert or public lawyer this would be the situation twelve months ago, they never would have believed you.
- From a Human Rights perspective, balancing the right to life with the right to associate, and the right to family life, is a precarious act and it is right to scrutinize every measure in that context and be skeptical of them to make sure they are not going too far.
- Once restrictions are taken for temporary emergencies, a look at history shows that they tend to become permanent (The Patriot Act from 9/11).

With COVID-19, the danger is that if it never leaves us and it continues to mutate or a different virus arrives with a similar dynamic, we'll be in a semi-permanent state of "this is what we do." When this happens, we have lockdowns, masks, emergency laws, more censorship, and of course, the ultimate: more vaccines.

It was a trade-off on the safety of the Covid vaccines as stated by Fauci but It is not a trade-off between the economy and lives. There are definitely connections between economic conditions and public health conditions. It is unprecedented.

Because COVID-19 is far less dangerous to the young than it is to the elderly or immune-comprised, and because generalized lockdowns are economically devastating, many countries have implemented targeted policies instead.

Aside from these rather obvious measures, and given new information that asymptomatic spread of COVID-19 seems to be "very rare," especially outdoors, the cost-benefit to locking down particular activities may very quickly decline.

Policies Targeted To Senior Centers

Here is a look at steps that weren't taken:

- Protective gear for workers at senior homes
- Do not send infected patients back to senior homes
- Do not rotate senior home staff
- Having senior home staff live on-site for periodic intervals for the duration of the epidemic.
- Bring in all necessary protective PPE/sanitizers for LTC.
- Government-provided funding for extra staff/extra protection instead of closing businesses
- Aggressive protection of the vulnerable and high-risk people
- Bring in the military much earlier
- Allocate resources to prevent overcrowding in hospitals

"While we should take the outbreak seriously, we mustn't panic and behave in a manner that is disproportionate to the threat we are confronted with," said Annelies Wilder-Smith, a professor of emerging infectious diseases at the London School of Hygiene and Tropical Medicine.

Countries Implementing Limited Lockdowns

It became a mad rush by governments acting on limited science. Then, science was about to get its turn at supplying public figures directing and dictating to politicians. There was, however, an opportunity to exert power with executive orders, lockdowns, takedowns, and jail time.

Economists know all too well this connection exists. They uniquely ignored this connection in order to support this policy blunder.

Ventilator Violence

Dr. Cameron Kyle Sidell emergency, a medical specialist in New York, stated, "I think we are killing people with ventilators."

The ventilators seem to be starving the patients of oxygen. He felt that it was quite sure the ventilator was not the full solution. He could not morally agree to continue with the current protocols in place.

From the American Journal of Respiratory and Critical Care, it was noted that Italy, the epicenter of the major outbreak, was not so much respiratory in nature. Nothing on mainstream news could be heard or seen, and New York fell into its own misgivings and tragic events with ventilators. In fact, Facebook and YouTube labeled this as false information.

Dr. Cameron was demoted and under scrutiny by the political powers of the hospital—until NIH stepped in and agreed with Dr. Cameron on April 21. The NIH put out a bulletin three weeks after Dr. Cameron reported the problem with ventilators, insisting that hospitals stop using them as much as possible.

Lockdown Insanity

WHO's special envoy on COVID-19, Dr. David Nabarro, sent shockwaves across the globe after repeating the same warning from countless other medical, legal, and economic professionals, including The Great Barrington Declaration, by calling for an end to the use of lockdowns as a primary way to curb a pandemic, and reminding us all of the sobering reality lockdowns bring with them.

It seems like we may have a doubling of world poverty by next year, and we may well have at least a doubling of child malnutrition. Children are not getting meals at school because the people who are in poor families already won't be able to afford it.

This may turn out to be a global catastrophe, so we really to appeal to old-world leaders to stop using lockdown measures as the primary control method. Few people could have imagined last Christmas that in three months, it would be illegal for them to leave the house.

Yet, lockdowns have become so normal that it can be easy to forget what an extreme and unusual policy they are. They curtail people's freedom and can harm almost every aspect of their lives.

In the broadest sense, however, this is very difficult to know for sure. "Lockdown" has already meant many different things in different times and places, which makes it hard to generalize.

In total, considering all the effects on healthcare, the economy, and people's happiness, the lockdowns we've experienced caused more harm than some of the alternatives—but it will take years to know the full effects of what we did.

For now, a detailed government estimate suggests that locking down in the spring did save many thousands of lives, compared with doing nothing, largely because it prevented the health service from being overwhelmed.

Lockdowns simply cause more harm than good. A strategy of "focused protection" of high-risk individuals, as set out in the Great Barrington Declaration—although in the opinion of the government's scientific advisors, and many experts in the field, this strategy would not work.

Do lockdowns actually stop the virus anyway? No, they just slow it down and delay the problem, allowing the virus to mutate.

According to the International Labour Organization, "1.6 billion informal economy workers (representing the most vulnerable in the labor market), out of a worldwide total of 2 billion and a global workforce of 3.3 billion, have suffered massive damage to their capacity to earn a living.

This is due to lockdown measures and/or because they work in the hardest-hit sectors." According to the World Food Programme, a quarter of a billion additional people will be pushed to hunger and 300,000 could die every day. These, too, are pandemics that are killing people. Killing cannot be a prescription for saving lives.

Health is about life and living systems.

New World Order/Build Back Better Narrative

What exactly are they building back better?

One senior official at the Department of Health and Human Services with deep ties to religious conservatives objected to any controls on church services.

"Governments have a duty to instruct the public on how to stay safe during this crisis and can absolutely do so without dictating to people how they should worship God," said Roger Severino, the director of the Department of Health and Human Services' Office for Civil Rights,

- Domestic violence is up 25%.
- Hundreds of thousands of children may die this year as the economic impact of our response has deprived them of basic medicine, food, and clean water. Tens of millions will likely fall into extreme poverty. This disproportionately impacts children from low-income families.
- Economic recession and reduced tax revenue always result in cuts to health services and hospital staffing. Those living in rural, low-income communities and third-world nations will be most impacted.
- Rises in unemployment during large recessions lead to reduced income, additional stress, and unhealthy lifestyles—all of which leading to shorter lifespans. A 20% unemployment rate could result in tens of millions of years of lost life.

- The truth is that children and the poor will be most severely impacted by our response to this virus. Many more of them will die and suffer from the fallout. The reality is that we are killing more people with our response than the virus ever could. More lives will be lost. The quality of life will be diminished. Dreams and lifelong investments will be destroyed.

What Is A Coronavirus Death?

In many countries, anyone who supposedly died of COVID-19 had simply tested positive but suffered additional health issues. The Italian Ministry of Health reported that 96% of COVID-19 hospital deaths had been with patients with severe underlying illness.

The WHO estimates that there are 300,000 to 650,000 global flu deaths each year.

Once you test positive for coronavirus and whether you have any symptoms or not, you are now on record for life as having coronavirus, and unless the registries change, your death will be marked as coronavirus, no matter the true cause?

Eyes Wide Open

Did people go to hospitals? It became increasingly clear that people did want to go to hospitals due to fear—even when faced with life-threatening events. Patients with diabetes or hypertension were no longer properly treated.

In 2017/18, a winter influenza epidemic swept over the world, and hospitals in the US were overwhelmed. Tents were erected, operations were canceled, and patients were sent home. Several states declared a national emergency. No pandemic declared!

Fear-mongering spread across the globe, and anyone challenging or defaming government or science would be censored. Every province, state, region, and city had its own rules and measures of what could be done or not, and many of these rules defied logic.

Human Dignity Vs. Human Life

Can you balance one against the other? The global economic consequences will be felt by all countries. After all, it is estimated 300 to 500,000,000 people will be thrown into poverty.

The government estimates that Australian suicides are already up 50%.

- 75,000 more Americans have been driven to alcohol and drug abuse.
- Regular admissions to emergency care have dropped from 20 to 40%.
- The mild symptoms of a heart attack are now routinely ignored for the fear of going to the hospital and catching the virus.

This list could go on forever.

Tens of millions of surgeries elective surgeries were postponed or canceled around the globe. What is the impact on the health of those people? And yet the justification was the narrative - "But we saved lives".

- Hundreds of thousands of children may die this year, as the economic impact of our response has deprived them of basic medicine, food, and clean water. Tens of millions will likely fall into extreme poverty. This disproportionately impacts children from low-income families.
- Current unemployment trends are likely to result in tens of thousands of additional suicides by the end of the year. These will disproportionately affect low-income families and those already struggling with mental illness.
- The truth is that children and the poor will be most severely impacted by our response to this virus. Many more of them will die and suffer from the fallout than from the virus itself.

It's easy to accept the extreme restrictions that our governments have levied and scoff at those who dissent when you live a life of privilege, but the reality is that we are killing more people with our response than the virus ever could. More lives will be lost. The quality of life will be diminished. Dreams and lifelong investments will be destroyed.

We're on the river of Niagara and we can hear the sound of the falls approaching and here we are with the captain who doesn't know what he's doing and has no awareness. Panic.

The politicians and the taking extreme and disproportionate measures because of "the science" and the projected models that were not only correct at the time but have been found to be totally absurdly incorrect.

Does anyone understand economics? The government bailout to keep businesses and people afloat is absurd. No government in peacetime has borrowed more money than now, and no government in peacetime has taken the liberty to destroy so many industries and jobs but still can continue to pay the people—in a sense as a cover-up.

Employers learned that there's no need to supply an office for you to work in as they attempt to recover from the economic damage. You are now under contract by the government and work from home. Only those that have had this happen to them will understand.

Censorship and separating the truth from the facts will become more widespread. There are going to be people that cannot tolerate the truth because if they believe this, that forces them to question their beliefs. To question the authoritative figure, we believe looks after our interests.

And now, to make matters worse, America is about to embark on a battle to immunize the entire country and world against COVID-19. This time, everyone is paying attention to the topic of vaccines. Everyone is searching for information. And the online, networked factions that have long fought to erode confidence in vaccines recognize that this is their moment.

Social media takedowns are not the right approach to addressing this content because they turn the propaganda into forbidden knowledge, often increasing the demand. Down-ranking and deprecating anti-vaccine content can minimize some of its reach, but it doesn't address the underlying lack of trust in institutions, pharmaceutical products, or government.

Restoring that trust requires far more work, but time has run out. The coronavirus vaccines are new, without years of data about efficacy or long-term effects. They have also been politicized,

Even during the 2020 campaign at the national debates, Joe Biden and Kamala Harris expressed concern about receiving a vaccine that the Trump administration and Warp Speed project were trying to achieve in record time. Did they think Trump was making the vaccine?

Warp Speed was an "all hands on deck" initiative with the support of countries around the world sharing information, engaging research labs, scientists, pharma and their mighty resources, and government all making financial and human resources to do so.

The gulf between the wealthiest and poorest had been increasing even before COVID-19 destroyed the globe's health and economies. The World Bank predicts the number of people in extreme poverty will increase by 100–150 million in 2021 alone.

Welfare programs were often criticized as unable to deal with economic changes, such as the threat of automation and the rise in flexible work. However, since March 2020, rising inequality and drastic changes to the labor market have forced governments to implement economic initiatives, such as basic income programs that previously would have been politically untenable.

New Zealand/Australia

Prime Minister Ardern was quick to "thank" the New Zealand "team" of five million workers for being kind and keeping everyone safe during the pandemic. Ironically, she is thanking them for something they had no choice but to do without breaking the law. What a good ploy: get the public to think they had a choice and then thank them for being good "children".

Apparently, this approach appeals to people who have a craving for strong parental figures.

The NZ government ran one of the strictest lockdowns in the world despite a low case number. It credits the lockdown for keeping the death rate at twenty-four even though more and more evidence shows lockdowns do not solve pandemics.

Lockdown

The COVID-19 pandemic containment phases really have not worked.

Many policymakers don't have the courage to ignore the panic and rely on facts. Leaders should and must examine accumulated data to see what has actually happened, rather than keep emphasizing hypothetical projections; combine that empirical evidence with fundamental principles of biology established for decades; and then thoughtfully restore the country to function.

Fact 1: The overwhelming majority of people do not have any significant risk of dying from COVID-19.

Empirical evidence, although a moving target, estimates that the fatality rate if infected is a risk far lower than previously estimated and in fact 85% of Covid cases will not require hospitalization (WHO).

In New York City, an epicenter of the pandemic with more than one-third of all US deaths, the rate of death for people eighteen to forty-five years old is 0.01%, or 10 per 100,000 in the population. On the other hand, people aged seventy-five and over have a death rate eighty times that. For people under eighteen years old, it amounts to 0.0002%.

Of all fatal cases in New York State, two-thirds were in patients over seventy years of age; more than 95% were over fifty years of age; and about 90% of all fatal cases had an underlying illness.

In the confirmed COVID-19 deaths that were fully investigated for underlying conditions, 99% had an underlying illness. If you do not already have an underlying chronic condition, your chances of dying are small, regardless of age. And young adults and children in normal health have almost no risk of any serious illness from COVID-19.

Fact 2: Protecting older, at-risk people eliminates hospital overcrowding.

We can learn about hospital utilization from data.

WHO reports noted that 80% of all cases were mild, and more recent studies show a far more widespread rate of infection and a lower rate of serious illness. Half of all people testing positive for infection have no symptoms at all. The vast majority of younger, otherwise healthy people do not need significant medical care if they catch this infection.

Fact 3: Vital population immunity is prevented by total isolation policies, prolonging the problem.

We know from decades of medical science that infection itself allows people to generate an immune response—antibodies—so that the infection is controlled throughout the population by "herd immunity."

Indeed, that is the main purpose of widespread immunization in other viral diseases—to assist with population immunity. In this virus, we know that medical care isn't even necessary for the vast majority of people who are infected. It is so mild that half of the infected people are asymptomatic.

That has been falsely portrayed as a problem requiring mass isolation. In fact, infected people without severe illness are the immediately available vehicle for establishing widespread immunity. By transmitting the virus to others in the low-risk group who then generate antibodies, they block the network of pathways toward the most vulnerable people, ultimately ending the threat. Extending whole-population isolation would directly prevent that widespread immunity from developing.

Fact 4: People are dying because other medical care is not getting done due to hypothetical projections.

Critical health care for millions of Americans and Canadians is being ignored, and people are dying to accommodate "potential" COVID-19 patients and for fear of spreading the disease.

Most hospitals abruptly stopped "nonessential" procedures and surgery. In Canada, as of May 2021, Health Canada has stated there are 420,000 procedures that will take a minimum of three years to catch up. That prevented diagnoses of life-threatening diseases, like cancer screening, biopsies of tumors now undiscovered, and potentially deadly brain aneurysms. Treatments, including emergency care, for the most serious illnesses, were also missed. Cancer patients deferred chemotherapy. An estimated 80% of brain surgery cases were skipped. Acute stroke and heart attack patients missed their only chances for treatment, some dying and many now facing permanent disability. The list goes on.

Fact 5: We have a clearly defined population at risk who can be protected with targeted measures and they weren't.

The overwhelming evidence all over the world consistently shows that a clearly defined group—older people and others with underlying conditions—is more likely to have a serious illness requiring hospitalization and more likely to die from COVID-19.

Knowing that, it is a common sense, achievable goal to target isolation policy to that group, including strictly monitoring those who interact with them. Nursing home residents, the highest risk, should be the most straightforward to systematically protect from infected people, given that they already live in confined places with highly restricted entry.

The appropriate policy, based on fundamental biology and the evidence already in hand, is to institute a more focused strategy like some outlined in the first place:

Strictly protect the known vulnerable, self-isolate the mildly sick, and open most workplaces and small businesses with some prudent large-group precautions. Healthy people should not be lockdowned.

This would allow the essential socializing to generate immunity among those with minimal risk of serious consequence while saving lives, preventing overcrowding of hospitals, and limiting the enormous harms compounded by continued total isolation. Facts matter. Healthy people should not be lockdowned.

12 The Endgame

"Let food be thy medicine and medicine be thy food."

—Hippocrates

- Missed Opportunity For Health
- Therapeutics Suppressed
- End Game Disruption

Chapter 12

COVID-19 is not something anyone of us wanted but here it is. It is real. How we managed it is surreal. It's worse than a bad movie about a rogue virus. It's like . . . Can this really be happening? But don't worry. The government has our best interests in mind. It will look after us while following "the science."

Covid brought so many of us first-time experiences of isolation, fragility, and loneliness while teaching us how the vulnerable need protection and causing us to reconsider the immune systems, RNA, T-cells, censorship, economic hardship, and every other impact caused by the lockdown. An unwarranted lockdown. We now have a culture of all ages being spoon-fed by government. The indoctrination of 5-year-old children wearing masks preparing them for the vaccines to come. And they are coming. A vaccine that does not prevent disease and wears off in six months will need multiple boosters already being prepared.

Of course, we saw the government power trip like never before, displaying record incompetency amidst the so-called crisis, each governing body looking to what other governing bodies were doing and making their decisions accordingly—decisions sadly based on fear. Flip-flopping and hypocrisy became the new normal. We didn't expect science to be perfect. Nor did we expect the government to be perfect. But here we are, experiencing absent knowledge and ignorance by design.

From a forward-looking perspective, there will be positive outcomes from all of this. There always are in any breakdown or crisis.

Every mainstream news media has been repetitive with the same narrative on COVID-19. Never before have we listened to such a morbid presentation every hour from media about the number of cases and deaths. Each year, around the globe, 55 million people die. Would you like to listen to the breakdown of 82k daily deaths? What about just the new cases in Canada and the US which see 4400 diabetes diagnosed everyday?

We have never started our day with the number of new cases and deaths from tobacco, heart disease, cancer, car crashes, etc. How shocking and morbid that would be, yet people listened every day to the number one news this narrative has been delivering for over a year and a half on cases and deaths. Clearly enough, this is a fear-driven agenda but to what end?

Fear-mongering has been the drive while incentives to get the vax have gone from a doughnut, a beer, a joint, a cruise to a lottery to name a few. Every vaccine dose gets us one step closer while you protect your community. Now, the health advisors are acting like a child molester on a street corner, advising government to lure children with candy, ice cream, narratives to keep others safe, and that it is cool to get the vax—which looks like perverted propaganda right in front of us. What's worse is that many parents are good with it while others don't have control because the wisdom of our health advisors give approval to a twelve-year-old to make their own decision. When you look at the stats there is a 0.00004% chance that a child will die or even transmit the virus. This decision is devoid of any real science and totally unethical. The propaganda machines are running on full tilt, pushing out a myriad of guilt narratives. If you don't get the vax, you could kill Grandma.

The fact is Grandma and the vulnerable should have been protected, and that is the government failing. A billion-dollar campaign with an agenda to keep the momentum going, and now you can hear twelve year-olds thinking it is cool to get this even more, six months plus vaccines are coming. Leave our kids alone. Why not pause the vax?

What if the vaccine fails us? Do you know how adverse events are treated? First, these vaccines had known limitations right out of the starting gates. Then, when COVID-19 mutates, another experimental vaccine will have to be produced. The variants will be blamed and so will the boosters.

As the vaccine rolls out, we will continue to listen to the same dialogue about the variants to get the jab to everyone—not science-based evidence to have six-month-old babies to eleven-year-olds vaccinated in order to protect the vulnerable.

Before Covid: How To Vaccinate 8 Billion People

If it is not fully understood yet, Pharma and collaborating partner's agenda is to maximize a huge opportunity to vaccinate the globe. For a successful global mass vaccination campaign to be successful, a lot of partners need to be in play to make it work. You first need an incidental highly transmissible virus. Then, you ignite a fear factor based on science models that show decimation larger than the Spanish flu. Ensure that past learning experiences from the other outbreaks regarding therapeutics, masks, and protecting the most vulnerable are fully forgotten. In fact, suppress any use of safe therapeutics for early treatment and do the same for alternative science opinions

Have an Emergency Use Authorized experimental vaccine never tried on humans somehow already on a shelf to start clinical trials in just six weeks after the first lockdown. To make it work, the fear factor needs to continue so. have the government overuse their authority with lockdowns. Use mainstream news and big tech to produce a narrative and censor anything that even hints as negative towards vaccines or other therapies as misinformation. How could that possibly work? Well, it is all shaping up to be a major test on our freedom, seeing how our rights so quickly removed against our Constitution or Charter of Rights. The move for vaccine certification is really the starting point for surveillance and the opportunity to enforce past and future vaccines in a new 8 billion marketplaces.

The World Economic Forum website talks about the Great Reset. "You will own nothing and be happy". This Great Reset governments are talking about should have been a lot more about health. An immense opportunity has been missed for the healthcare systems and governments around the world. Our immune system is nature-dependent, not vaccine dependent. Every aspect of decisions made by health advisors and the government have amounted to a complete disconnect.

For 600 days, few words were spoken about health. This was truly an opportunity that has been missed. Natural health has been smothered by the only remedy—a vaccine. Nowhere was the thought to bring a new refreshing narrative to all about healthy eating—the power of the sun, nature, a garden, and maximizing the essential nutrients, minerals, and vitamins for a healthy lifestyle that keeps your immune system positioned as the strongest defender against viruses and disease.

Sadly, no. In fact, the very opposite has happened. Lockdowns, staying indoors, allowing the virus to replicate, not protecting the vulnerable, economic destruction, worrying, fear, and stress all contributed to the exponential impact of this virus and creates other health issues. The psychological impact of masks not only on ourselves but in shunning others who didn't wear one.

The guaranteeing of the healthy is not in the playbook of how to manage a pandemic. But that was abandoned overnight. Even worse no cost benefit analysis on a lockdown was done at the time or now. What makes sense is sick people should be quarantined and the vulnerable protected. Other healthy people didn't need to be locked down. Yes, healthy people did test positive, but the statistics overwhelmingly showed which groups (in terms of age and comorbidities) COVID-19 targeted.

Is it not our government's job to look after our health? Why are they manipulating the narrative to mandate a vaccine when 98.98% majority are not impacted? It's a complete contradiction when they allow you the choice and freedom to smoke tobacco. Yet tobacco has a death rate fifty times this virus which is absurd and dwarfs what Covid has done. Again, no alarm bells.

We have the freedom to eat what we want. Nutritional guidelines are set out every few years, but you just need to look at their sponsors who are influencing public health. It's not just Pharma that is indemnified. The US Cheeseburger Act protects food manufacturers from people who accuse them for their obesity. About 40% of our food labels are not correct. Food products that have been designated carcinogenic leading to cancer are listed in recipes of the Heart and Stroke Foundation, American Diabetes and the world's largest organization of food and nutrition professionals. Is it possible people are confused based on these guidelines what healthy eating is?

In 2016, the FDA gave a ruling to allow food companies to add new ingredients into food products without any notice to the FDA or the public. This is the same FDA that granted Emergency Use Authorization to a first ever mRNA vaccine and soon to be granting the same for the boosters and the move to get under 12 vaxxed.

Therapeutics

Why was there a complete global shutdown of therapeutics? There are so many drugs that have been repurposed for other conditions. If there was a safe drug that could reduce hospitalization or death wouldn't you want to know about it? There was a concerted effort to block hospitals, clinics, and doctors from using other safe approaches as preventative therapy. The Association of American Physicians and Surgeons have a guide[25] for early treatment to Covid that has shown in 85% reduction of hospitalizations and death. Again, no alarm bells! See the footnote to download the treatment pack. My experience with my personal Doctor stated he could not prescribe any therapeutic or refer me if I got Covid. There was no advice to use natural health to use Vitamin D, Zinc, Queritin and others as natural immune protectors to help against Covid.

These treatments were not emergency use authorizations like the vaccine. They were not new drugs just released. But the missing requirement from Tony Fauci was they did not have randomized

[25]https://aapsonline.org/covidpatientguide

double-blind clinical long-term studies as an early treatment preventative. Wait–neither did the vaccines but they got green light with EUA.

There were thousands of doctors around the globe who have spoken out and who followed their Hippocratic Oath "to do no harm". They did not stand by and watch their patients suffer and die from Covid by using proven safe therapeutics as early treatment with huge success. Like 85% to 100% success. This information has been reported to the FDA and to Congress but not on mainstream media.

Hydroxychloroquine has a 65 year old track record and over 78 studies worldwide that show it's safe and effective against respiratory illness. Doctors around the world have used it as a treatment for early infection.

Five years ago, Tony Fauci described successful studies about its antiviral and anti-inflammatory capabilities on our respiratory systems. Those that use it in their medication for example in malaria-plagued African nations appear to be the least affected. What about immune-compromised people with Lupus that take Hydroxy? Interesting no major impact from Covid with this group.

June 4, 2020 - The online prestigious medical journal The Lancet has apologized to readers after retracting a study that said the anti-malarial drug hydroxychloroquine did not help to curb COVID-19 and might cause death in patients. The Lancet does not retract often, and for that retraction to happen there must be strong evidence supporting HCQ. What that means is the success from doctors who used it as early treatment should have been recognized resulting in saved lives.

BioMedCentral (BMC), a pioneer of open access publishing, published an article of their studies in Virology Journal: that chloroquine had strong antiviral effects against Covid.

In the meantime, there were many clinics and doctors around the globe that had great success with HCQ, Zinc, Quertin[26], and Vit D with their patients. On March 23 2020, Dr. Vladimir Zelenko reported that he had treated around 500 coronavirus patients with HCQ and had seen an astonishing 100% success rate. That's not the "anecdotal" evidence Dr. Fauci sneers at, but actual results with real patients in clinical settings.

[26]https: //www.youtube.com/watch?v=k8RyV3VEDKI

Governor Andrew Cuomo, who sent Covid patients back to their LTC homes banned the use of HCQ in the entire state of New York, and other Democrat governors of Nevada and Michigan soon followed suit, and by March 28, 2020, the whole country was under incarceration-in-place. No hospital could or would prescribe.

Many doctors have said, "As a physician, this baffles me. I can't think of a single infectious condition—bacterial, fungal, or viral—where the best medical treatment is to delay the use of an anti-bacterial, anti-fungal, or anti-viral until the infection is far advanced."

- A Henry Ford Health System study showed such treatment to lower the death rate of COVID-19 patients.
- Officials with the Michigan health system said the study found the drug "significantly" decreased the death rate of patients involved in the analysis.
- The study analyzed 2,541 patients hospitalized among the system's six hospitals between March 10 and May 2 and found 13% of those treated with hydroxychloroquine died while 26% of those who did not receive the drug died.
- "As doctors and scientists, we look to the data for insight," said Steven Kalkanis, CEO of the Henry Ford Medical Group. "And the data here is clear that there was a benefit to using the drug as a treatment for sick, hospitalized patients."

Oxford University–(and Budesonide) the oldest university with high-ranking credentials has stated 90% of deaths may have been prevented. 9 out of 10 people in the early part of the pandemic who were put in the hospital died.

The conclusion of the study was early administration of inhaled budesonide reduced the likelihood of requiring urgent medical care and reduced time to recovery following early C19 infection

Professor Mona Bafadhel of the University's Nuffield Department of Medicine, who led the trial, said: "There have been important breakthroughs in hospitalised COVID-19 patients, but equally important is treating early disease to prevent clinical deterioration and the need for urgent care and hospitalisation, especially to the billions of people worldwide who have limited access to hospital care.

The vaccines we already know will take two to three years to reach everyone across the world. A relatively safe, widely available and well-studied medicine such as an inhaled steroid could have an impact on the pressures we are experiencing during the pandemic.

Even now, in this global health emergency circumstance, it's important not to abandon science. What's important now is identifying critical therapeutic targets based on our best scientific understanding of the disease process, assessing our existing arsenal of drugs to match up the best scientific fit to hit the target, and then efficiently assessing both the safety and efficacy of the drugs.

In the first 6 months of the pandemic, censorship took a stronger role. Rightly so. Every country had to deal with false and misleading claims regarding hundreds of Covid cures—from 5G to hairdryers to cocktail concoctions all willing to take money from gullible people.

Censorship now from Big Tech has gone too far in overstepping free speech and platforms for the masses and true voices to be heard. The conflict of interest is right in front of us as Big Tech companies are in the vaccine business and, given their partnerships with Big Pharma, any negative news impacts their bottom line.

Scientific debate has been shut down and you are only hearing one side of the equation. That one side has some elements of pseudoscience and quackery, and our politicians are buying it. Take, for instance, having natural immunity to Covid. One level of government is saying you only need one dose. What? While a higher level of government is saying you should get two because of the requirements of other countries if you travel. Natural immunity has always ruled over every vaccine made for human injection. It's madness. And of course, children who have a 99.98% chance of not getting it, transmitting it or being hospitalized. But to get to the desired government level of 80% vaccination, more ice cream will be needed.

The trail of human and economic damage around the globe from this crisis, the lockdown, the removal of freedom and rights, the decisions from health authorities will be immense. How do you measure that? Perhaps only how it has impacted you and your family. This is usually about as far as most folks go to really understand the situation. Just get the vaccine and you will have privileges.

No one will know how the experimental vaccine will point to future chronic conditions because the vax does not leave a 'thumbprint'. The drive is to get the original placebo group to get vaxxed and therefore no long term gold FDA standard study. All future serious adverse events will be deemed there is no correlation with causation. What we do know is that reporting systems are telling an eerie story. In the US, data from Dec to July 2 from the US Vaers[27] system show a total of 438,441 total adverse events and 9,048 deaths. The European Union database for 27 countries for vaccine reaction reports is EudraVigilance. From Dec to July a total of 17,500 deaths and 1.7 million adverse events. Close to 50% happened within 48 hours after the vaccine. Again, no alarm bells or mainstream media reporting because correlation is not causation.

What will be hard to see and measure is the impact of lockdowns. Millions of procedures around the world put on hold. Global poverty increased by 25%. Standard vaccinations globally decreased by 22% What about those lives not being saved from disease. Some smart people will map that out and the low number of deaths caused by the after affects of Covid will be 100 fold to that of Covid.

The questions are coming out and there will be more. The Informed Consent Action Network provides true information that is hard to find and often harder to understand. Through the freedom of information Act, they have thousands of Tony Fauci emails[28] now available on their website. His emails are now showing that many truths are being exposed. Perhaps, exposing known therapeutics that could have saved lives. He is already under scrutiny by Congress on how he coordinated NIH funds to do corona virus research at the Wuhan Lab. The National Institute of Health involvement, masks relatively ineffective, PCR tests are only 50% accurate, exchanges with Facebook about where resources would help. The Children's Health Defense has been exposing the corrosive impact of corporate power on democracy, censorship and protecting the health of children.

The truth is that this pandemic is not the endgame and should be an awakening for everyone. It is also continues to be a moving target.

[27]https://childrenshealthdefense.org/seeking-justice/exposing-the-truth
[28]https://www.icandecide.org

That medicine and science has become crucial in everyone's lives but as a nation we can no longer pretend our trusted agencies are protecting us, the vulnerable or our children.

It is your duty and responsibility to yourself, your family and your community to replace fear with knowledge to become informed and educated. The truth about vaccines in the last year and a half have had more exposure than the last 20. Pharma already has plans to bundle six vaccines in one shot to sway public opinion that 90 doses by the age of 18 may be too much. Variants are quite natural but they will be used to keep the narrative moving until everyone buys into the free flow of vaccines and then they move to the next phase. The vaccinations for 25 and under should stop until science can prove there is risk. Only one child to date in the US has directly died from Covid. The risk is 0.00001% of death. Bee stings are higher.

The real End Game is for everyone to realize government is slowly removing our rights, our freedom and you can turn off mainstream news and use alternative news as your new programming. That blind trust with drugs manufacturers and one size fits all vaccines need to be questioned. We all need to advocate for our children and not to take for granted the science is correct. Follow the science now means follow the narrative. Just take the vaccine and you will have freedom.

Years ago, one individual 'took a knee' for his belief and was persecuted. Well, look at how that became a worldwide acknowledgment of a statement for change. One person can make a difference and all it took was a symbolic knee.

About the Author

Ted's extensive background on cybersecurity led him to write a book; Bitcoin–The Unstoppable Force. One area described how embedded microchips with built in applications for transit, restaurants etc are already being used by thousands.

As he was researching the chemistry of drugs and vaccines for dogs along with processing of kibble has created sickness. The pandemic hit worldwide. The pandemic then switched his research into our vaccine technology resulting in a huge awakening. From being pro-vaccine to becoming pro-truth.

After 14 months of research on a moving target, it lead him to question, why the number of children who develop Autism was 1 in 10,000 decades ago and now it is 1 in 50? Since the 1986 Act that gives pharma indemnification from all vaccine injuries, the adverse events curve on a graph points only one way–up. No pandemic alarms here.

The lockdown had purpose. The vaccine target market is now 8 Billion people. Vaccine passports are in play paving the way for microchips that will come through with the 5G infrastructure. The stage is set for more vaccines to come and for our youngest children. Pharma, Bill Gates Foundation and the Big Tech who own vaccine companies will benefit. Censorship, information controlled by Big Tech, the removal of rights and follow the science narrative will continue. *"Just vax and you will be free."*

Made in the USA
Monee, IL
10 September 2021

76814084R00115